THE NEXT DIMENSION IS LOVE

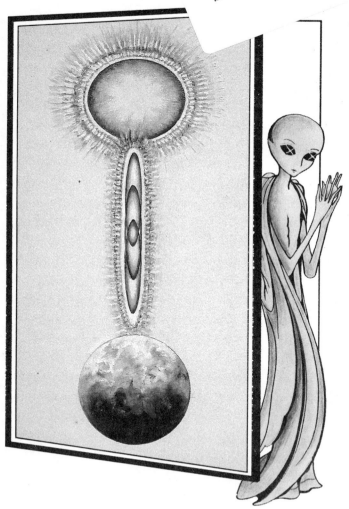

RANOASH the ATAIEN
CHANNELED THROUGH
DOROTHY ROEDER

RANOASH

the ATAIEN

Channeled by
Dorothy Roeder

Published by Light Technology Publishing
P.O. Box 1526, Sedona, AZ 86339

ISBN 0-929385-50-0
Library of Congress
Catalog Card Number: 93-080767

Cover painting on door by Tria Schwartz
Cover illustration by Michael Tyree
Cover design by Fay Richards

Printed by
Mission Possible Commercial Printing
P.O. Box 1495, Sedona, AZ 86339

Time for Healing and Transformation

An Other-worldly Look at Our Problems and Potentials
Channeled through Dorothy Roeder

Synopsis

Ranoash is a very evolved being who exists in a dimension parallel to our own. His world is so advanced that it has already completed this creative experience. Instead of returning to the Oneness, he and his people have chosen to remain in that world and to explore the past through it, expanding their knowledge of creation further. As our own consciousness expands, our dimension is beginning to touch theirs. These beings, who understand the power of love far more than we do, wish to share their knowledge of balance with us in return for learning what we of Earth have discovered about love. We have strengths, it seems, that they do not. They also have been asked, by the Creator, to help us heal ourselves and our planet. This book explains their perspective on what needs to be done and what we can do to help them help us.

The gathering storm
   The cleansing rain
      The Earth bright and new

Grown again from the seeds of the old.

◊

Planted with hope and love
   Seeds grow toward the light
      Roots reach deep into Earth

Direction, purpose come from within.

◊

Perfection evolves
   Mind manipulates, guides
      listens to the flow of growth

Taking it where it can see, hear, feel Light.

◊

Feeling guides from without
   from within
      moving with the perfect eternal flow

Becoming One.

1

My name is Ranoash of the Ataien. I am a friend of yours although you will probably never meet me or see me in your physical reality. I wish that were not so for I would find it very helpful for my purpose to be able to communicate with you directly. You see, we are so different that my appearance would be quite threatening to you, or so it would seem from past experience. We have tried many times in the past to contact you directly, but each confrontation met with disaster, often more difficult for us than for you.

My reality parallels yours. My people and I have experienced a development that is similar to yours in many ways. Our physical forms began evolving from one-celled organisms, just as yours did. As we evolved our consciousness and our ability to work with physical existence, we merged consciousness more and more closely with our physical form. As the body became more capable of supporting our consciousness we were able to bring more of our consciousness into it. This necessitated many changes in our physical forms during that process. They changed radically at times to accommodate the type of consciousness that we wished to express through them. The evolution of your bodies has been similar although you finally evolved a different type of body.

We have finally evolved into a form that is similar to your insects. Our physical appearance is that of a very large praying mantis. That species on your Earth was so named by the Greeks (mantis means divine) because it was believed to possess supernatural power. The belief arose out of a race memory of a time when we physically intervened to avert a catastrophe which was imminent on Earth. It was being invaded by aliens from another universe and the resulting disharmony created a severe disruption of the life-support system on our world. This was at a time when our worlds were "closer" dimensionally. They have since separated and now come together again. These aliens were threatening to invade our world also. They proved to be no match for us. While they were in your dimension, their mental powers were diminished. We were able to use our minds to immobilize them and then, when they refused to leave, remove them. We transformed their forms and consciousness into energy which was harmonious with ours, using it to heal Earth and repair the dimensional structures around our planets.

Humanity was not yet present on Earth physically, but was participating in its development through working with the more primitive forms which preceded development of human bodies.

You can imagine then how long ago this was. The aliens looked at Earth as very primitive, not understanding the complicated evolutionary process which was occurring, nor its potential. They were looking for food and power, and Earth had plenty. Such races with very primitive respect for life have long since been eliminated from this universe. They were the remains of creative energy which became totally disconnected from the flow of the Divine Plan. We have frequently served as protectors of the development of the Divine Plan. I will talk about that more later.

Unlike your insects, we do not prey on other life forms. Originally we consumed certain plant juices to survive, developing farming methods which were very efficient and supported the life of the planet as well as ourselves. Now we no longer need that. We can utilize light directly as energy, although we still enjoy eating physical food. We have wings although we do not need them to travel. We fly for enjoyment and in meditation. We would be about six feet tall in your eyes, and walk upright. Our color varies from light gray to medium gold. We become more golden as we age. Our age is difficult to explain because our dimension uses time differently than yours. We would be extremely old to you. We die only if we choose to and can usually reclaim our physical form if we so choose. We could actually choose any form, but find this one most harmonious with our life flow and place within the Divine Plan.

Like your insects we also have a very strong group consciousness which unites our individual consciousnesses into a whole. We are all capable of individual thought and accomplishment but are always aware of and guided by the needs and directions of the whole group. At times this has intensified our experiences together to the point where we have almost destroyed ourselves. Several times it took outside guidance to turn us away from our destruction. We welcomed this help and eagerly sought its assistance to develop solutions for our difficulties.

We have reached a point in our evolution now where we no longer need to explore these difficult areas. We have learned to see ahead into the directions we are taking and determine the probable future results of our present course. More importantly, we have learned how to stop moving in a direction that is leading to disaster and make the necessary corrections in our behavior to avoid them. This has allowed us to become very effective in analyzing the actions of others as well as our own.

We now spend much time as a group, sharing the loving ecstasy of Source flow. We sing together for days on end. We also share our thoughts as we maintain our world consciously. We have learned enough about the whole creative process that we directly control it ourselves on our planet. This is something that you are learning to do on Earth, but your creative processes are more complex and varied. Ours are the prototype for yours. You need our experience and the creative base we have built. We need to share your expanded opportunities for growth to complete the expression of our potential.

We possess the ability to travel in other dimensions parallel to our own. This ability we brought directly from Source. Unlike you, we did not have to learn it because we never forgot our unlimitedness. It is quite simple when you learn to open yourself to it. When you have freed your creativity from the limitations of pain and separation, you will be able to do it also. We will talk more about that in later chapters.

3

Again, this does not mean we are greater than you, only that we are exploring our creativity differently.

About one thousand of your years ago we began an extensive exploration of other dimensions. We do not at present travel forward or backward in time, but laterally. We have spent this time exploring, studying, and analyzing what was happening in these other parallel dimensions. That has so completely fascinated us that we no longer extend our explorations into the future, that being more and more available to us as we explore the present. The last five hundred of your years we have spent discovering the imprint of the past in present reality . We have seen that most often the future is revealed quite clearly by study of the past.

We record what we learn on computers that are much more advanced than yours. They are biological in nature and capable of growing and repairing themselves as needed. The most outstanding improvement is that we can record our thoughts directly onto the computer record without having to use some physical means of connection into it. We have only to organize our thoughts and "send" them into the computer. In this sense the computer is an extension of our consciousness, but we do not need to retain that connection unless we have a purpose that requires it. We can dissociate from the group consciousness of our people if we wish but we very seldom do so unless in a process of very intense thought. Such concentration of mental energy can be disruptive to the group consciousness as it sometimes draws too much energy into one point. The intensity of the thought flow can create a warping or even a discontinuity in what you call the space-time continuum. The thought of just one person can draw others into the flow of that thought if it is powerful and directed enough and create sudden discontinuities in our stream of experiencing.

We eventually learned to direct our very concentrated thinking out of the group consciousness when the vibrational level of our thoughts exceeds certain limits. This disconnection is directed by our subconscious minds much as your physical body controls its own temperature. Various physiological and psychic loops provide both the feedback and the control mechanism that allow the process to occur without our having to be concerned with it consciously. We have learned to override the process consciously through mind development, but we have also had to learn to take moral responsibility for this action and it is not now done without consent of the group.

But we are not computers. We are individuals with free will just as you are. The fact that our minds are "linked" into the group of our immediate kind does not limit our actions to the will of the group. We are so aware of the results of each of our thoughts and actions on the whole, we do not usually do anything to upset the balance there. We have learned to create together a flow of life and thought that creates harmony for the whole. This harmonious flow allows us to each work at his or her maximum creative potential. As individuals we each have unique ideas but as part of the group those ideas become available to the whole. The group can decide how to use each new idea and whether or not it is useful. Each one gives up some control of how his or her idea is used but gains the creative contribution of the group in deriving maximum benefit from it. This adds diversity to the whole while maintaining harmony. Perhaps you can see that this sort of group integration of the individual would be helpful on Earth.

We were compelled to work in this way to stop the destructive competition that had been destroying us and to find a more productive way of working. This competition was not destructive in the physical way you have competed on Earth, but conflicting thoughts were preventing the cooperation within the whole which allowed us as a group to achieve our purpose. Once we had each given up individual claim to our creative flow, we began to discover that creativity comes from the Creator as a "seed" which grows in diverse ways according to the "soil" in which it is planted. Depending on the wishes of the mind which grasps it, it can be applied on many levels of consciousness or into many situations. New concepts, if truly divinely inspired, are available for all who are open to them and are interpreted by each in a unique way. You might recognize this lesson as one that would be useful for you.

We have learned to recognize that our spiritual guides receive new ideas in the same way from the higher creative-organizational levels, resulting in a flow of each new idea throughout all of creation. Our purpose in life has become one of allowing this creative flow to come through us and we are one in our desire to connect with the highest, purest form of creative thought.

At one time in our history we thought it necessary to purge the group consciousness of individuals whose thoughts did not harmonize with the flow of the whole. We eventually discovered that we were no longer evolving as a group. We were locked into a fixed loop of experiencing, unable to break out into the next level. We realized that we need some diversity of thought and action in order to move forward in our ability to use our creativity as a group. We then entered a long period of trying to integrate and balance what seemed to be disharmony into a group consciousness that was sufficiently balanced to allow some continuity in our lives. Some of the more radically different ideas were set aside, not discarded, until they could be evaluated for usefulness by the group. This restricted change to some extent but still allowed the group to maintain a productive balance.

There have since been occasional individuals who felt their ideas did not fit in and that their creativity was too limited by our safeguards for the whole group. These left our group and sought one that would allow them to carry out their ideas without the controls we would have imposed. They looked for groups that were willing to allow other ideas to be integrated into or imposed upon their energy system (their world, for instance) to carry them out.

There are many dimensions of experience parallel to ours that are available to us. Most are regulated like ours to provide the level of balance that has been agreed on by the group. Others are so chaotic that nothing can be accomplished. There are some in between these seeming extremes that allow more divergence from the norm than ours. Your Earth is one of these. So some of these "radicals" from our group have joined you, sometimes creating chaos in your world, and sometimes great leaps forward. At the time they left we merely observed that they had gone. When we learned to travel through dimensions other than our own, we began to pick up the trails of these cross-overs. We began then to discover the price we had paid for balance and harmony in our flow of experience. We appear to have eliminated some opportunities for exploring the higher potentials that your race has gone into, although we have gained much strength from unity. We do not now feel we missed something in choosing the plan of group evolvement that we did, and we want to explore the results of the diversity which we gave up for the time since.

The diversity we gave up and which crossed over to Earth has manifested on Earth in subtle ways that are much entangled with cross-overs from other dimensions besides ours. Your Earth has sought for some time to be open to and supportive of all who sought to find a place for their creative ideas. She has not limited them in any way, simply trying to find, as best she could, a place or a group where each would fit in. The situation as we see it is reaching a critical point where there is so much diversity, chaos is imminent. It is time to begin the process of harmonizing all that diversity.

America became the prototype for doing that on Earth. About the time we began studying the variances in the flow of parallel dimensions, you began seeking some way to integrate your individual patterns of desire into a more harmonious flow for the whole. Those who wanted to try out yet another new idea, this time one that would allow individual creativity to flower and still support the whole in balance and harmony, began the movement to a "new world." We observed this and began to look for a way to help you by sharing our experience and knowledge of balancing group energies.

So, enough about us. I want to talk about you and how we can work together. The purpose of this book is to introduce ourselves to you so you will understand who we are and what we are doing. Most of you who read this book are beginning to realize that you need a new viewpoint for healing yourselves and your planet. While much of what we say here has been said before, we hope to show how we can help you heal yourselves. We have knowledge that you have forgotten and we want to show you how to regain it yourselves. We come to you with much love and great respect for you and your Earth. We have always supported your special purpose in the Divine Plan and hope to help you more successfully fulfill it.

Ranoash of Ataien

2

Interdimensional travel is not difficult when you have control of the mental processes that create reality. As we began to learn to do this we were contacted by beings from a dimension other than our own who helped us. They said that as our minds began to open to possibilities outside our own experiencing, an energy flow was created that began to draw new experiences to us. We developed a magnetic flow that literally drew toward us what we needed to expand our concept of ourselves. This magnetic flow attracted the thoughts (for thoughts are but energy flows also) of beings who were able to find us by following the path of the flow. They were more developed mentally than we are now, but they responded to our potential for expansion much as we are responding to yours now.

As your mental abilities have created great expansion in your thought processes in the last one thousand years you have been generating an energy field around Earth which is beginning to reach beyond what you know of yourselves into what is unknown. It is this ability to face the unknown and welcome whatever it may bring that creates the opening we needed to contact you. You are calling out for new connections to bring you new ideas and higher levels of understanding about life itself.

We began to try contacting you at your conscious levels, but your inability to accept anyone in a physical form other than your own was new to us. As we projected ourselves into your environment, through the power of our minds, we expected you to understand that the physical form was not important. You have not. Buried in the physical matter of your bodies' cells is a belief that any form other than your own is inferior and dangerous to your survival. We are amazed that even very small differences in form cause you much difficulty, differences such as size and shape of nose, not to mention skin color. Your minds cannot grasp that the inner spirit and the quality of your thoughts determines your worth.

Even those of you who think you are quite accepting of everyone can be very judgmental about appearances. This caused us much difficulty as we tried to answer the call that was coming from Earth. You either could not see us as we really were because your minds could not form a true picture of us, or you were so terrified that we were in grave danger for our lives. Many of us have been killed when we tried to contact you directly and your minds are so closed to the experience that you did not even know what had happened. You simply developed a fear of something that related to something already familiar, such as insects, in our case. This is not completely true for everyone, but the numbers of humans who can accept us in physical form are many, many fewer than you might think.

So we have been forced to hold ourselves back and wait until you are ready to receive us. We have chosen to contact you on dimensional levels where you can accept us, but these levels are rarely completely conscious even when you can handle some knowledge of us. This is unfortunate because there are many beings other than ourselves who are responding to the expansion of your minds and who would like to help you, teach you their special knowledge and simply be your friends.

We do see that this fear of different forms is something that your Earth is seeking to conquer at a very basic level of creative purpose. It is as if Earth selected for her body atomic material that had great intrinsic love of being physical. This love of the physical is a great source of physical power, but it has not allowed any opening into its use. It is as if that very strength prohibits its own expansion, forcing it always back into itself. The love locked into the physical plane must be released before you can use it as power to achieve Earth's purpose. It must expand into new experiences and new ideas.

Earth's basic elements make up your cellular structure and so you contain the problem and the potential. The difficulty in opening up is limiting you in creating a physical form that will allow you maximum use of your developing minds. It is not the particular form that is limited but the way you see it. You see it as the final perfected form, but it is final and perfect only for this moment. The form must be flexible enough to allow expansion at any moment, be it great or small. You have to struggle with your physical form for every bit of expansion in yourselves that you allow. Your forms are of a much higher energy level than they were one thousand years ago, but so much sickness and pain have accompanied the struggle to attain that energy level.

Many of you came to help Earth out of this misperception that physical forms are sacred as they are and cannot be changed. You came from dimensions or times where you knew better, but became trapped by the immobility of form as soon as you entered it. You have now concluded that the solution is to surpass the form, to grow out of it and leave it behind. But this does not allow you to use the inherent power in physicality and make it part of yourself. This was demonstrated quite clearly by your use of atomic power. You all believed at conscious or subconscious levels that that power must create destruction of the physical form. You are searching now for another viewpoint because that obviously was a very destructive path, but you still struggle against your subconscious and conscious misperceptions about physicality.

We have decided that the best way we can help you is to help you transform the physical bodies that hold you into your belief system about what life is. We are trying to help you expand your minds beyond your present perceptions about being physical into new ways of using the physical resources that your physical bodies and Earth's offer you. Your Earth is moving into a higher, more radioactive part of space. You will not survive as a race if you cannot learn to evolve your physical bodies along with your minds. We believe that the Creator has some purpose in creating physical forms and that we are obligated in some way, by choosing to be in them, to develop them to the fullest. We can influence your bodies with our minds from our dimension, so we are able to facilitate change on Earth without your conscious knowledge. However, we are now mindful of the harmony and balance of the universal flow just as we have learned to maintain balance and harmony in our own group. We now know we cannot make changes in your dimension without your cooperation. It upsets the harmony of the universal flow, so we do not do it.

We have studied your progress, the potentialities of your present path of evolution, and as far as possible your purpose for being here. We have conferred with our own cosmic, spiritual guides and yours. We have been contacted finally by your galactic sector and asked to help you specifically. We have undergone training with those who are responsible for organizing the forward movement of this galaxy. We have also allied ourselves with beings from other dimensions, times, and spaces who are also willing to help you in response to the call you have sent out.

Finally, we have studied your way of doing things and integrated, as much as possible for us, the purposes of your dimension into ours. This is done by "reading the records" of your purposes which are available to those who choose to facilitate the universal flow. Access to these records is available through special permission of specific persons who work at higher dimensions of your Earthly reality, namely the fifth and sixth. A group of "librarians" maintains them, as well as the history of your dimension and your communications with other dimensions, parallel and vertical.

I mentioned before that the Earth is coming into a higher-energy portion of space and time. The new conditions resulting on Earth from this energy field are necessitating specific changes in your physical forms as well as in your emotions and minds. Your mental bodies have been adapting to the faster flow of this energy field better than your emotional bodies. However, the flow itself is now moving your emotions so much that it is becoming easier to allow them to begin to take on the new form. You have realized consciously that this is necessary and the conscious mind can then help provide the structure of the new emotional consciousness that is required. You are learning to be more free within yourselves so that your true emotions can flow. These are joy, truth, freedom, peace, allowingness, acceptance, and most of all, love.

Your physical bodies, however, are not changing because of your beliefs that the form you have now is superior to any other. There needs to be a change in your conscious belief system about your physical bodies. When you can see the ideal form as part of a continuously evolving opportunity to explore physical existence most efficiently, rather than as an end in itself, it will be better able to support you through all types of physical experience.

Your physical bodies have not always been as they are now. You know a little of that history from your science of evolution. They have been evolving lately to allow you to experience through your expanding mental abilities. When your mind was very rudimentary, your body was different. Your minds are now reaching the limit of their abilities to function to their maximum capacity within the present physical form. Your minds are reaching beyond the form into time and space. You need a body that can support that, but can your present physical body allow you to go outside of yourselves as you are presently using it? Some of you have solved this problem by learning to go outside your bodies — astral travel, you call it. This can bring much information that helps in the transition period. But what is really needed, if physical existence is to remain a part of your learning, is a body that can itself move into other dimensions and realities. The physical form must not be limited to this particular reality if you are to expand your physical consciousness outside this one.

The Divine Plan has taken all this into account; at least this is how we see it and how it has been explained to us. Somehow, this Plan provided an expanded energy field just as you finished learning to use the old one. It has also provided you with the help and guidance you need to exist within it. The basic plan of evolution for your physical form is encoded in the Light that comes to you from the Galactic Center, which coordinates all levels of the Divine Plan and makes it available to the various dimensions which are governed by it. We have seen some of this as we, ourselves, learned to exist consciously in more than one dimension. We have also been taught by our spiritual teachers who can see and experience even more at the higher dimensions than we do. I have not directly experienced everything that I am telling you here, but as I become more adept at contacting other dimensions while remaining in this one, the higher ones seem to be more available as a part of the lateral dimensional movement. In other words, lateral dimensional movement itself seems to naturally produce vertical expansion into higher dimensions and vertical movement opens up lateral opportunities.

Focusing directly on the vertical possibilities, however, seems to take one out of physical reality. The higher dimensions are so exciting and expansive that one seems to become lost there and the physical perspective is lost. We have observed this phenomenon on your Earth. Most of you believe that anything physical is inferior to what you call "spiritual." Celibacy is more spiritual than sexual activity, for instance. Priests are more respected than farmers. Earth is dirty and sky is clean. (At least it used to be until your refusal to look beyond your immediate physical desires changed it.) To you, sometimes, anything is better than life on Earth.

And yet your divine souls have chosen to live and experience here. They look at physical existence as a great opportunity, one that they have been working to create, even in its present form, for eons. Is your distaste for physical existence the truth or is your soul's perspective clearer? Well that is for you to decide. For our part, you are in physical existence, miserable, sick, and exhausted from your struggle with it. Things will get worse as you move more deeply into the new energies and attempt to hold on to the old form. Yet you are all choosing to experience it and even clinging desperately to it, so we assume you have some reason for having physical bodies. We want to help you transform them into ones that support you rather than limit you.

We are willing to work within the form provided by your sector of the Galactic Center. As I said, the "blueprint" for your form is encoded in the Light that comes to you from there. The code is retrieved in various ways depending on the level at which you are working. It is, however, already a part of each unit of consciousness within the governing field of Light which it uses. The ideal for every form you have used on Earth and every form you will use is coded into your consciousness somewhere. The appropriate form is emphasized and brought into play by the influence of the galactic Light. The galactic Light "turns on" each new level of development at its appropriate time. That is a mystery which we do not yet completely understand although we have seen it happen many times in ourselves as we studied our own evolution and in others as we work with them or their history.

One thing we are quite sure of. Where dense physical existence is concerned, the Light codes have not been enough in themselves to produce transformation and have always gotten help from other levels of consciousness and outside dimensions. The flow of evolution seems to get stuck when it goes through physical matter and the Light does not seem to be able to unlock the new levels at the correct time without help from other dimensions, vertical and horizontal. This help is seldom invoked from the level of physical consciousness. It comes from the soul level or as part of guidance, often forcefully imposed, by those entrusted with the flow of evolution, through other physical beings.

As a result the changes imposed by the requirements of the new form meet with much resistance from the physical level. Many terrible wars have been fought on your planet, before your recorded history, to drive away these agents of change. I grant you, they did not always come with a great deal of sensitivity and understanding for what you were experiencing. And often, their own ulterior motives were more important to them than your comfort, happiness, and understanding. Beings who possessed that ability to be empathetic to your feelings were not always available at the physical level needed for working with you. But your conviction that your form is best, wherever it is, is a difficult obstacle to overcome.

Consequently, your physical matter on Earth has much buried resistance to change and many memories of violent attempts to injure or alter your physical bodies. Every battle against change has seeded more resistance to that change into your physical cells. Change must now be created in a way that does not allow your conscious physical awareness to interfere and activate your resistance to change. If you put this together with the absolute necessity to allow the changes that will allow humanity to continue on Earth as it moves into this higher energy field, perhaps you can begin to see the necessity for methods now being used to help you.

I am speaking about what you call "abductions by aliens." Your minds are programmed, by those violent memories of alien invasion and slavery, to resist any contact with them or us. If we can contact you in a state of consciousness which is somewhat disassociated from your physicality, we are often able to communicate with you in a fairly agreeable way. Even that does not always work and your fear is such that it would disrupt your life. We do not want to do this, so we erase the memory of our contact with you.

This system is not working as well as it used to. The new energy that the Earth is experiencing is causing the dimensions to overlap and run together more and more. You are becoming more aware of other dimensions that occupy the same time and space that you are using. The fact that you now, in some sense, are becoming aware of us in your space makes it harder to erase your memory of our space. Your space has become ours and we cannot cut you off from your own space. We need some way of helping you to accept us as a part of your space even though you see us as very different from yourselves.

Also, this new overlapping of dimensions causes them to affect each other more than before. The hate, anger, and confusion of your Earth consciousness is beginning to upset the balance of our group consciousness. We must find a way to help you balance your physical reality so we can maintain the balance in ours. You will not be able to accept this help fully while you are locked into the belief that your form is superior and more important. And you will find it difficult to change your consciousness while your physical bodies remain resistant to the changes that will allow you to evolve beyond your present level of experiencing as a group.

Our task is to facilitate the physical changes. Other groups are working with helping you to change your consciousnesses and expand so you can accept as real more of what is not physical. This book is an attempt to help integrate our task into your understanding of your whole evolutionary flow. It is also an attempt to make our work a little easier. If you understand consciously what we are trying to do, perhaps we can communicate more clearly in the way that you would choose, even though you do not yet fully accept the necessity of our intervention in your evolution. Your emotional bodies resist us more than your mental bodies. We want to be able to work with you consciously without manipulating your minds against your will. Your enlightened mental comprehension of the process can help your emotional selves to understand and cooperate.

We are learning much through working with you. We have gained from you as a result of our efforts and I will talk about that next. No one in creation, so far as we have seen, ever serves without gaining something for one's own knowledge and evolution, for that is the purpose of existence.

Ranoash of Ataien

3

I told you before that we had not allowed some things into our experience which we now regret missing. One of these is emotions. We know love and we value that more highly than anything else we know. But we do not feel the many varied ways in which love can be expressed. It may be hard for you to conceive of this, but we do not feel joy or belonging as part of love. When can we observe and share your emotions, your joy reflects to us as love. Negative emotions such as anger or hate reflect to us as lack of love, even though to you they may have been motivated in some way by love.

We cannot, we feel, derive as much learning from love as you because we cannot experience it in so many different ways. You learn about love through joy, peace, compassion, trust, allowingness, truth, loyalty, harmony, right action, expansion, understanding, and many other qualities, but most of all through wisdom. We know that we have wisdom, but not having developed it as a specific quality through study and experience, it does not bring us the expansion of consciousness that it does to you. We brought the quality of wisdom directly from Source as we individualized, where you look at it as part of your Sourceness which you must reclaim. Not having recreated it within ourselves, it does not take us deep into the ultimate flow of love as your wisdom can. You have had to dig deep and search hard for each bit of your divine wisdom and can see more clearly its ultimate value.

Love, for us, assures us that we belong, that we can communicate with others in the ideal way, or that we have available the knowledge we need from within ourselves. It does not allow us to feel the divine ecstasy that you feel when everything is aligned within you. We can realize the rightness of the flow but you can derive so much more from it, which allows you to magnify the flow and use it in a greater way as creative power. You have a potential for expansion that we lack because your ability to use the flow of love in more ways gives you greater potential for using divine power.

I know you are thinking that emotions are not always such a good thing. They can be very difficult and can seem to take the place of the love you want to feel. But when you have solved the problems associated with emotions and have learned to use them to express love you have learned more than we ever will be able to. Once you have turned anger into right action, judgment into acceptance of the beauty of diversity, or grief into joy, you know more about love than you did before. When you learn that you can use this energy as a clear flow of love through your physical body you will no longer feel pain.

It is through twisting the flow of the Creator's love into something negative that you experience pain in your bodies. We do not feel pain because to not allow that flow of love would be to not accept life itself. Since we missed the opportunity to learn how to feel love in the diverse ways you do, we have not had to learn to use each quality in the way that allows it to express love. We simply accepted the love as an absolute, incontrovertible fact and allowed it to be a part of us. So we do not experience pain. We do not have pain to show us when we have taken the wrong path, we only have cessation of life.

This does not mean that we have never done anything wrong. We spent eons "experimenting" with our life force, using it for our personal gain as well as using it in harmony with the flow of the whole. Taking it out of the harmonious flow of the Creator's will caused us to become dissociated from it and to lose our physical body or whatever part of ourselves we were using at the time. We had to then recreate our body, for our divine purpose kept directing us to be physical and try again. We repeated this individually and as a group many times, learning, finally, how to use our life force, which is the Creator's love, in a way which results in harmony and balance. When we are in harmony and balanced we know that we have taken the correct line of action because we can maintain the flow of our lives.

You have broken love down into many individual components, and explored them individually. This allows you to maintain a partial connection with the flow of the life force that is love which supports your life, even though you make mistakes and use part of that flow in ways that are not in harmony with the Creator's will. You focus intensely in one aspect of love, perhaps to the complete exclusion of all others, thinking that that is the most important. Whole societies on Earth have been devoted to one "truth," such as courage, loyalty, joy, or devotion. This ultimately created an imbalance which caused the society to destroy itself or be destroyed, but you will have learned much about that particular quality and also how it must fit into the whole of yourselves.

You have all done this enough times that you know a great deal about many of the qualities of love. You also are seeing that it is not enough to use only one — all must be available in abundance when needed. As the new energy field creates an acceleration of your lives, it also creates an acceleration of the flow of your experiencing both past and present. The threads of your past experiences are coming together so that you must deal with great part of your knowledge all at once. Once you had the leisure to fit the pieces together slowly and carefully, focusing, perhaps, on the blending of joy and movement, or devotion and loyalty. You could blend the knowledge from a few lifetimes into a flow that made sense. This allowed you to make the corrections that erased past mistakes and allowed you a clear use of these particular qualities of love.

Now many, many lifetimes are coming together with their incomplete knowledge and the guilt of past mistakes, and you must deal with them all at once. There is no longer any time to explore joy as a solitary goal. It must be balanced with peace, abundance, communication with others, everything. It must, in fact, express the highest degree of love that you have accepted as a part of your life. It must allow others as much joy as you have or you cannot feel right about being joyful. You are trying to integrate all you have learned about love on Earth into one life which will allow you to express, for your Creator, the clear flow of Its love through you and through Earth.

This process of integrating all that experience into one short period of time on Earth is causing some imbalance and disorientation now, because it brings up for you what is incomplete as well as what is complete. And yet, the flow of these new, higher energies is ultimately directed toward integration and unity. They are taking you back into the harmony of the whole from which you originally came. The flow of Earth's progress through this new energy field promotes the integration and peace you are looking for. If you can align with it and accept it, it will take you to your goal. If you cannot, you will be left behind to deal with the chaos you created by your mistakes.

The key to this alignment is inside yourselves. The seed of your wholeness is buried in your hearts and begins to bloom as you learn to integrate love into your lives. For you, you must integrate all the aspects of love that you have explored. Each one of them is a piece of yourself that must eventually "come home" to the whole of what you are. Your misuse of each aspect of love must be resolved into a clear understanding of what it is and how to use it for the whole, yourself, the Earth, the universe. As your pieces fall into place, your ability to use love creatively, in alignment with the Creator's Divine Plan, grows magnificently and explosively.

Do you begin to see the potential within all of you on Earth that we see? Nowhere else in this galaxy is there such potential for expansion of the Creator's Plan through love because you know more about love than so many of us. That is what has attracted us to you, more than the chaos of your struggles and disharmony. This coming together of the energies of your potential is creating a vortex of power that can be useful, ultimately for the whole of Creation. Many groups such as ourselves are fascinated by the possibilities here. We would like to share something of what you have gained.

We know that you have much work to do yet before you are able to use love on Earth in the way you would like to. Even though we have evolved somewhat differently, we feel that we can help you in what you are trying to do. Perhaps our more sure conscious knowledge of ourselves as an aspect of the Creator's love can help you regain the balance you have lost. Perhaps the balance and harmony of our society can help provide some stability in yours. We are willing to risk some loss of our balance in exchange for a chance to share your knowledge of the many ways of experiencing love.

Some of the healing you are doing on your physical body involves its ability to be integrated with the emotional body. Your emotions, more often than not, are the key to your illnesses and pain. I am not saying that sickness or pain is all in your head. That would be to say they were caused by thinking. It is not your thinking that causes most of your suffering, but your feelings. It is emotion that creates the intense surges of energy that magnify certain of your experiences into pain. If you have a violent experience that involves much anger, hate, or fear with the injury, emotion magnifies the energy of the experience so much that your body can no longer handle it. Your body becomes overwhelmed and some injury or loss in the physical is the result.

If your mind and emotions remain balanced during the bad experience, you do not lose the sure knowledge of your spiritual power and you remain in control of your body through the experience. The injury is not magnified by emotions and the healing processes of your body can work in the ideal way. Your mind becomes a helper in the process and the emotions allow the healing energy to flow properly. You can remember all the right things to do. If you continue to fight out of anger or hate you are not supporting you body's needs. You are intent on focusing your anger on another rather than focusing healing on yourself. You take the energy you need to heal yourself and send it to another as anger and hate. The negative emotions and the pain become locked into the cellular memory, creating a loop that reruns the pain whenever that memory is triggered. Some of your creative power is diverted into maintaining that loop and is not available for your higher purposes.

That is just one example. Have you ever had the experience of pain, where thinking about something else takes your mind off the pain, or where being depressed or sad makes it worse? Have you, on the other hand, ever been so intent on something that you did not even know you had been injured, then when you noticed it, the pain began? Pain is a function of the emotional body in that the mind itself does not feel pain. It only receives the message, sent by your physical body and magnified by your emotional body, that you are hurt. Then it refocuses your power flow back into the pain, magnifying it.

Notice that "hurt," as I used it there, can have meaning for the mind or the emotions. Emotional hurt is just as difficult to deal with as physical hurt, maybe even more so. The word hurt is a symbol for injury that can be interpreted in several ways. Your subconscious does not make distinctions without conscious help. When you say to yourself, "I am hurt, I am in pain," and you feel much emotion about suffering that pain, your subconscious begins to create pain in as many ways as it can. It will keep creating pain as long as you give it the emotional energy and mental direction it needs to do so. A great key to releasing yourselves from pain is in releasing yourselves from the undirected, unrestricted use of emotion. Conscious understanding of the sources of pain allows you to begin to learn to use your emotional energy creatively for the Divine Plan rather than to create pain for yourself. Love, wisdom and self-confidence are emotions which can be directed to an injured area for healing

Emotions are not the only key to banishing pain from your lives, but it is important enough that I feel I must discuss it as part of the healing process that we are trying to facilitate. Also, although your abilities to feel emotions are a strength we would like to learn, they are also the chief difficulty we have to overcome in reaching you. You have much emotional energy bound up in resisting what you consider intrusions into your personal space, and your bodies are the most personal space of all. This is part of that great belief you have that your physical bodies are the most important part of being alive. After all, that is in "reality" the only part of yourself that you can see and experience directly. But let's get back to healing your bodies by healing your emotions.

Every emotion is associated with some area of the body, localized or even very general. As it is reinforced through many lives it becomes crystallized into your cells as energy that does not flow and as a state of being cut off from the ideal that you want to express physically. These crystallized areas can be activated in many ways through repeated lifetimes. They can appear and disappear according to your emotional state at any time or they can last a whole lifetime, becoming more and more hardened as they are increasingly unable to flow Light. New emotions can become associated with them and they get bigger.

When the healing process begins and you begin to focus on these areas, you begin to release the energy that is crystallized and concentrated into them. The emotional flow that comes from them spreads all over any part of your being that will allow it. The flow may stir up other areas and awaken buried pain there. Your life can become a constant turmoil of pain and suffering if this process goes on in an uncontrolled way. Your emotions can be further stirred up by this process, creating more anger and frustration along with the pain of healing, so much that you just bury it all again. But you cannot keep burying it any more. The new energy flow, the higher energies themselves, will continue to bring it up and show you it is there. You cannot continue to exist here unless you are willing to look at all of what you are — pain and physical imperfection as well as Light and love. There needs to be some way to release the energy in the crystallized area without creating more pain for yourself.

The techniques we use to heal you involve directing energy in the form of the ideal that you wish to be. The ideal is always flowing, unrestricted, yet directed by a plan, ultimately by the Divine Plan of the Creator. You do not learn to consciously use the ultimate Plan all at once. You integrate it into your knowledge about yourself and your power bit by bit. We do not heal you all at once. We cannot. We begin with the area that is most likely to accept change at the time, consistent with your beliefs about yourself. Too much change could result in the complete disconnection from your physical body. For instance, if your only knowledge of yourself as a physical being involves pain and disease, you will not be able to exist without it. You must be allowed to release it gradually, learning that you can live without each pain as you release it.

As we begin helping you create movement in your being, the

energy becomes freed to align with the ideal rather than the imperfection. If you choose to immerse yourself in the emotional energy that is released and hold on to the pattern of the imperfection, progress will be very slow. If you can learn to allow the emotion to come up without again grasping it and allowing it to control you, you will be able to just let it dissolve and leave. What you will have then is pure energy, no longer forced into an imperfect pattern which creates pain, but yours to use to energize the ideal. We will discuss this more when I describe how you can cooperate with us in your healing.

There is a belief, common on your planet now, that your emotions are being stirred up against your will by beings who use that energy for themselves. In some cases this is true. Your use of emotions does have the capability of magnifying energy greatly. In our case, the activation of your "stuck" areas releases energy which we can use to heal you. If you choose to let it no longer be a part of your energy structure, we can use it for ourselves. I can assure you most sincerely that we would much rather use positive energies than confused, chaotic ones. It is much easier. We would like to help you learn to generate so much love, joy, and peace that you have enough to share with the universe. We would like to be able to share your positive emotions to stimulate our own latent emotional abilities so that we also could contribute more to this explosion of creative Light.

Do you really believe that any being, opposed to your spiritual purpose or otherwise, can create something in you that you do not wish to have in yourself? Do you believe that another can make you hate if you have only love? We do not see that anyone except yourself controls the quality of your feelings. If another being creates a situation that you connect with and that causes your emotions to rise, whatever emotions are already in you determine whether anger, curiosity, acceptance, fear or love comes up.

As part of the healing process we would like to help you transform hate into love, anger into right action, fear into trust, imperfection into beauty, chaos into peace, disharmony into balance, lack into abundance, all over your Earth. We do not understand how to create all of these qualities of love, but we do know how to balance energy and create alignment with the ideal. If you can learn to use a balanced flow as a basis for your use of emotions, we can combine our strengths for our mutual benefit. Everything is energy. Thought, conscious or subconscious, shapes that energy. Consciousness and knowledge of the ideal are the tools that can heal yourselves and Earth. We can help you align your consciousness with what we understand of the Divine Plan and help you learn to use your thoughts constructively.

To do this, your minds must be able to balance the flow of your emotions without inhibiting them, allowing them to flow with the shape of the ideal and energize it. You must learn to work with your emotions so that they support your thoughts, energizing them and carrying them to their destination. You need to learn to use all of your emotional power which you have built up for many lifetimes, including that which is now locked into areas of pain and imperfection. We will begin by helping you heal your physical bodies and release your emotions for positive purposes. Your own divine souls will provide us with the ideal and your minds with the conscious energy as we work together to make the ideal real for you and for all creation.

Meditation/Exercise

Get comfortable in a chair or lying down is fine if you don't fall asleep. Imagine a ball of golden Light just over your head that represents your soul and its cosmic connections, ready to be brought into the physical level. It is sending a beam of pale gold Light with many-colored sparkles down around you. It causes your heart to light up with as much of your soul's energy as you have learned to use. Know that you are receiving all the love that you can use. It is simply flowing to you unlimitedly, regardless of how you feel about yourself today, or how you think others might feel about you. It is always available to you, but right now you are taking time to enjoy it and know that it is there.

Inside the golden ball is the ideal for your body and your use of love as Light. Send a message into the ball that you would like to work with that ideal. If you have a special problem you can ask for a specific pattern relating to it. You might want to heal your heart at the emotional level. Ask for that. You might want to heal some part of your body that hurts or is not working properly. You can ask for the ideal pattern for that part. You might want to ask for help in recreating some area of your life, such as abundance or relationships. The pattern for each thing you ask for could have connections into other areas that you expect, so be aware of that.

Ask your soul to show you a symbol of the part of the ideal that you have chosen to work with. If you do not feel you are able to imagine what it is sending you, choose your own symbol; that will work just as well. Then imagine your soul flowing the ideal as the symbol with the Light from the ball, through the Light beam into your body, down through the top of your head, through its center, your throat, and into your heart. The symbol may feel at least a little familiar when it reaches your heart because the ideal is already present there. You are simply finding it and putting it to work.

Allow the golden Light to flow through the ideal as your symbol and radiate from your heart so your aura is filled with it. The symbol expands so that you are filled with the ideal and surrounded by it. Let it flow into your lower chakras and into the Earth under your feet. Now place it in the area where it is specifically needed. Let the Light flow in there and fit it in, flowing through it to make the appropriate connections into the rest of your body system. If you are not sure where to place it, ask you soul to guide it in.

Now that the proper connections are all in place, you are going to energize it. This is where we come in. You have chosen the area you want to work on and your soul has brought in the pattern which is best for you. Imagine your golden ball surrounded by more Light which flows through it into your body, bringing healing energy and whatever special help you need. As long as you keep the flow going, we can work with you to heal and transform your body. Allow your soul to bring in whatever help you need. There will be others besides us ready to help you. There are a host of beautiful, loving, spiritual beings all around you all the time, waiting for you to allow them to help you. Be specific when you ask for help, but allow that help to come in whatever form is best at the moment.

Let your imagination be free to know the many different ways you can receive help. Keep the Light flowing in and radiating back out from your heart and into the Earth. Allow yourself to know and maybe even feel the love, the joy, the caring that are coming to you through that Light. Focus into the peace and love and, as you end your healing session, try to find a way to carry them into your physical activities. This will help maintain the level of progress you have just made in the healing process. Every time you do this you will receive further healing.

Ranoash of Ataien

4

The relationship between the physical and emotional bodies on Earth is unusual. You spent much more time during your evolution developing it than did most other races in this universe. You used it most outstandingly during your Atlantean period but your development of it began almost at the time Earth was first formed, before it was completely physical. Normally — and I have compared Earth's development with that of other planets in this universe, about 10,000 of them — that level of understanding or energy use is simply a part of the energy structure which supports the physical level. The physical level is the goal, in that a body is needed only as a means of experiencing the culmination of understanding brought from all other levels.

The emotional body is used as a connection between the physical and all other levels of awareness. It is not an end in itself, but a means of reaching that end. The expression of love is not the goal, but a means of flowing the Creator's energy into new creations. The emotional body is then a mechanism for connecting love from these Source levels to the physical level, the physical level being somewhat dense so that it needs a special help in making this connection. The emotional body is then simply an extension of the mind which is the creative tool the soul uses to work at the physical level.

I am assuming here that you understand that everything is energy. All energy is electrical movement which flows from the creative center of the universe, which we are here calling Source or the Creator. This electrical flow arises from the intentions of Source as It conceives mentally what It wants to create. This concept is a specific focus within Itself which cannot include all of what It is at one point, because It is a process of isolation. This initial focusing or individualization causes a fragmentation of the Creator Itself into many smaller, incomplete cocreator-creators who partake of the qualities of their Source but who cannot express them as fully and clearly as the original Source.

Each cocreator-creator contains a part of the original thought which began the process. They are connected through the flow of that thought which is motivated by love, and consists of love because love is the essence of what the Creator is. We are not speaking of love as something that specifically makes you secure or makes you feel connected to another, although love certainly can do that. We are speaking of a cosmic concept which is the uniting principle of the universe. Everything is pure, unconditional, infinite love for all that exists — the Creator's love for Itself. This love binds All together through Its awareness that all is love and nothing can be separate from it. Love is the unifying force that holds the universe together even though that universe may be splitting into fragments in numbers approaching infinity.

This flow of love can be regarded as electrical because it consists of individual particles of energy, thought impulses, moving toward a goal, the Creator's purpose which was conceived in the initial thought. Does this reduce each of us to a minute speck being propelled toward some unknown goal? No, because we are part of the Creator, individualized by its original thought. We are a part of the creative process that cannot be separated from it, since the thought generates the form of everything that exists. We are a part of the original Creator which is developing or expressing the thought. Each part expresses it a little differently, each one proceeds toward the goal in a special way that is unique. Therefore, each one has a different set of experiences which comprises its learning process and becomes unique in its development of the original thought.

This creative thought develops until the Creator, through all Its cocreator-creators, completes the thought and brings it to a conclusion. The process is one of initial fragmentation and then gradual integration and merging as the thought completes itself. What does the Creator think about? Itself, of course, there is nothing else. Each of us is a small part of the Creator, exploring all we know about ourselves through thought which flows as love. As we move through creation and explore it we must gradually discover that we are not separate and that each one only appears to be different from another because we are expressing an individual aspect of Source. We do learn to see similarities between ourselves and others and eventually can begin to see Source in each other. As we learn to recognize these similarities we are drawn together by the love which is the essence of what we are. Our knowledge of ourselves literally causes the resolution of the initial thought, because love is the cohesive force that makes us all One.

This particular creative idea, or universe, has reached the point where resolution of the original thought has begun. It is coming together. Love, transformed through the creative cycle, is producing a flow back to Source. Everything we have learned about ourselves is being integrated into larger and larger pieces of the whole. Love binds the pieces together and draws more to it always. Love is such a strong binding force that it seems now to be drawing to it more than was a part of it originally. It is drawing more creativity out of us than we originally had. We and Source are growing because love is the force that moves us through this exploration of ourselves and also creates expansion.

The emotional body has developed as a part of yourselves which connects you into this universal flow of love and can lead you us back to the group, the integration, the final goal. When it is aligned with your heart, the emotional body is the part of you that recognizes flow. As it has learned to work with your heart, it has learned to recognize whether or not this flow is a clear part of the universal flow and one that will lead you to your individual goal. It serves as an indicator of the correctness of your actions, your thoughts, and the "direction" of your movement. If your movement is toward more love, the movement is easy and keeps increasing. If your actions take you out of the flow of the whole you feel separation. Eventually you learn to follow the direction of the emotional body with less and less concentrated effort and you move automatically and consistently toward the creation of more love. Your emotional body becomes an automatic pilot which leads you to your goal. Can your minds do that? I think not, because thought was the initial cause of the fragmentation of the Creative Source. Mind seems to have created the impulse to explore yourselves, while love has created the knowledge which ultimately puts the pieces back together again. Mind allows you to learn more about yourself while emotion keeps you in touch with what you really are.

Now what happens when love itself is fragmented into pieces? For one thing, many more potential paths are created for exploration while the cohesive force of love is apparently diluted and the paths separated from the whole. This is impossible in reality because you are Source and cannot be separated from what you really are. But your emotional body becomes fragmented. Part of it holds you to the individual path which was created out of love and is recognized as leading to some necessary goal. This goal, however, seems incomplete. It leads to confusion and separation. Another part remains connected to the whole and tries to lead you back to it. What you have then is a divided body which seems to be working against itself. This division is multiplied many times, once for each path you have taken and not been able to integrate into the whole. The more paths you take, the more fragmented your emotions become. The more aspects of love you explore individually, the more separated you become, not only from the Creator, but from your self. You have become so fragmented you no longer know who you are. Your desire to learn more about love has seemed to take you further and further from the expression of what love really is.

This fragmentation has occurred mainly at the physical level. You do not experience such overwhelming feelings of separation when you are not in your physical body. Your physical body has become a prison that holds you into separation from your true self and keeps you from being part of the whole. But it was not intended to be that. You originally took physical bodies so you could bind physical matter into

34

the whole of the flow of Universal Love. And you wanted to be a part of the physical level in order to experience completely the merging of physical matter into the Universal Flow. You had experienced these merges into the flow at other levels of existence and they were exhilarating. They showed you things about yourself you had never dreamed of. They created in you power and movement beyond anything you had thought possible. So you decided to separate love into as many fragments as possible, because wouldn't that then give you the biggest possible "bang" in merging?

Well, you got in over your heads and created such fragmentation of yourselves that you have been having a hard time putting yourselves together. Like Humpty Dumpty, the task looks hopeless. The only solution seems to be to give up on physical existence. It was a bad idea anyway, right? Even if you try to reclaim something of the physical you might have to do it without the emotions, because they got you into this mess to begin with. Does that strike a chord in you? The emotional body seems to be a pretty weak and useless tool to use to put yourself back together. And yet, it is the only one you have that can reclaim your physical experiences and give them value. It is unfortunate that your minds have decided they are the ultimate tool for your salvation. They simply lead you into more fragmentation of yourself. Minds can categorize, analyze and discriminate, yes, but by themselves they cannot connect into the big picture of the goal of wholeness that you are seeking. They need an emotional body that is whole and strong and able once again to lead you unerringly toward the path that leads to wholeness. Your emotional body is the connection to the flow of universal wholeness.

And your ability to use love in your life at the physical level is your key to allowing your emotional body to lead you back into wholeness within yourself. As you become whole, as you integrate your pieces, you can allow love to guide you to your goal, even while you are in a physical body.

We said that you use the emotional body differently on Earth than we do. You decided to split love into many components for greater understanding through experimentation and exploration. You had to fracture the emotional body in order to deal with the different aspects of love. Just as the physical body became an end in itself, so each aspect of love became an end in itself, requiring sometimes a separate personality structure to deal with it. This process began before the evolutionary process led you into a physical body, when you were still going through the fourth dimension, on the way to becoming physical.

We are having to condense the story of creation rather severely here. Briefly, you began as an aspect of Source, without any kind of form. As you looked at the Divine Plan and your purpose, you gradually acquired a form that allowed you to express that purpose. At first the form was simply a pattern of consciousness. Slowly it began to accumulate matter of increasing density, concentrating its enormous power into more and more specific forms. It was billions of years before you reached the level of Light that you can now feel or perceive dimly at what you call the astral level, or the fourth dimension.

Each level of concentration of energy and more specific form took you further from the infinitely expansive flow of love. It was not possible to concentrate infinity into a focus on one aspect of that flow. Some were able to maintain some awareness of unlimited love, but many lost the ability to be aware of that and your special focus at the same time. You sensed the separation from the Source flow and began to look for ways to reconnect with it. From your viewpoint of looking at individual specifics you could see only part of the flow of unlimited love. You were right in deciding that you had contacted it, but not entirely correct in thinking that that was all there was.

This led to a habit of thinking that the way you were progressing, the path you were on, was the correct and only one. Then you would work with the aspect of love you had connected with, reach the end of that path, having gone as far as you could with only part of the truth, and feel betrayed that somehow you had been misled by love. There was an enormous feeling of loss that you had not been able to reconnect with the unlimited flow of love and make that part of yourself again. So you began over with a different aspect of love and repeated the process. Each dead end created a misperception that that part of self must be in error as it did not lead you to the goal. So you became a collection of pieces that didn't seem to fit together and work.

As you moved more into the physical, third-dimensional level, you began to see how to integrate the various aspects of love into one. Physical bodies seemed to help because they tend to hold on to the patterns of past experiences and produce a certain amount of continuity through their tendency to prefer old patterns. They maintain some of the meaning of the previous path gained before you reached the dead end and the misperception of error. You learned to hold on to some of the wisdom gained along each path and could use that in your next attempt to move forward. This has produced a great deal of forward movement without much appreciation of where you have been.

As you move into this present time of integration, these "old paths" are coming back to you. But they bring not only unfinished business and old mistakes, they bring the knowledge and strengths gained through them. Because, you see, the physical level is not the only one where you learn. When each path ends you have time to study its conclusions outside your physical consciousness. Your soul and your spiritual teachers and guides have a chance to help you decide what was gained, as well as what did not work. You do not often remember this when you are again in physical consciousness, but you will have set up a group of opportunities to use the strengths and integrate them into your understanding of self while you continue to work on the more challenging aspect of your potential power.

We are a part of the strength you are now integrating, part of the self-awareness. Once we were a part of you and your evolution. You chose to explore love in its many expressions as specific goals. We chose to use love as the unlimited source of opportunity to learn about ourselves. We could not remain together with these seemingly opposing goals so we separated so completely that we could no longer remember the others existed or that they had any validity for existence at all. Then the inexorable progress of evolution began to bring us back together again. We can no longer pretend that you do not exist or that we can remain separate from you. And, you need help if your species is to continue to evolve. If you continue on your present course your race will cease to exist. I am not referring to the fact that it is still possible to destroy your Earth or at least make it unable to sustain life. I mean that your bodies as they exist now cannot maintain life in a changing universe, in the presence of the new energies which are ultimately your source of life.

Your present bodies are fighting the new energies, trying to maintain the present form against the flow of evolutionary progress. Your illnesses are not just the result of emotional disconnection from your wholeness. They are the result of fighting change. As long as you cling to the idea that your present form is the ultimate, perfect vehicle for expression of the God within, that God is doomed to cease to exist in physicality. You will have reached another dead end, this time at the physical, not the emotional level. If you still want to bring the ultimate Light into physical existence on Earth, with its great promise of fulfilling all your dreams for physical existence, relinquish the conviction that the integrity of your present form is all that matters at the physical level. Allow yourselves to see that this form is merely a transition to another which will help you learn more about how you might express your creativity through form.

Your path was not more right nor more wrong than ours. It was simply different. If we work together, we can share what we have learned, combine our forms into one that will make the next stage of galactic evolution an opportunity to learn together and become more of what we ultimately are by our coming together again. This is our goal and I am offering this book to you as a proposal that will help all of us to stay in the evolutionary, creative flow. We cannot continue to evolve without you, because without the evolution of an expanding consciousness there is no creative flow.

Not only is your inclination to create chaos and separation a danger to our existence. We need the strengths in using love that you have developed to reach the next level. We have also reached a dead end in our experiencing. Our love is complete but not broad enough in our understanding of what it is to allow us to make use of the coming level of evolution. There is no further reason for us to exist. We can make no use of this new level that is appearing now. And yet we can see great creative possibilities within it. The choice you once made to turn from wholeness into separation now becomes ours as we ask to help you put your pieces back together. We realize that we risk losing some of our balance and wholeness, but we also see that you have made much progress toward releasing separation. We think and feel that we can maintain a stable point of reference for you as you continue that progress.

As we continue to help you with the healing and transformation of your physical bodies, we ask that you accept us with love even though we are much different in form and temperament. For our part we admire greatly the strength of purpose you have in pursuing your course of Earthly evolution. We do not always understand you, but we want to learn all we can about you so we can begin to share our knowledge about what we are in the divine sense. We want conscious feedback from the physical level about how we can work together. We have it now from your more spiritual selves, but we are interested in working out our merging at the physical level. We already understand each other at the spiritual levels. There was never separation there. We feel a need to extend that understanding to the physical level. Help us by being open to what is unknown and not understood. Stop looking for evil in whatever is not understood and look instead for an opportunity to learn and expand.

We do not expect immediate solutions to our problem of contacting you in a friendly, cooperative way. We do hope that many opportunities such as this book will gradually open your minds to ideas that are now inconceivable to you. As your minds open, your hearts will open and your emotions will flow in harmony with our love and our purposes, as well as your own divine love and purposes. We will find ways to explore our individual purposes together and help each other. The more we do this, I suspect, the more we will discover how much the same we are and how much our goal is the same.

I do not believe that we were meant to remain separate. I believe that we took separate paths in order to finally blend them into a higher understanding of the experience of creation and our potential.

Next, I want to talk more about how you can facilitate our working together and our understanding of each other.

Ranoash of Ataien

5

Our planet is quite third-dimensional; it is as physical as yours. We are not figments of someone's imagination, nor are we ephemeral. Our bodies are solid physical matter which you could touch and feel. Our world exists in the same space as yours but in a parallel dimension. Your dimension and ours are like two train tracks following the same path but never touching. This analogy fails in that we are not identical physically. As I said before, at some higher level we are very likely very much the same, but if you were to see us you would not find any point of similarity in appearance except that we both have a body, four appendages, a head, and stand erect.

When our worlds separated, each began to follow a different path. Some parallel purpose has kept us close but separate. We are not sure what that purpose is, as divine purposes are too abstract and vast for us to grasp with our physical consciousness. When one looks at the details of that purpose from a more cosmic perspective the focus on those details which physicality allows is lost. The two viewpoints can only be resolved at the physical level and understood at the cosmic level. The understanding can sometimes be grasped intuitively with the physical mind, but is then difficult to hold on to or put into words. Words are too limiting and our physical minds not broad enough.

Many of us on our planet have began to understand intuitively that our continuing presence depends somehow on yours. If the path of one of us should end, the other will cease to exist also. Somehow we each provide an anchor in physical reality for the other. It is not the same sort of balancing as Light and darkness; that is another matter, another parallel. It is a balancing of energies that requires the existence of all of us. At one time we felt that as a group, our planet was ready to ascend and move to a higher dimension, one that flowed at a higher electrical vibration. When that did not happen, we began to look for the cause for our remaining here. We did not feel angry or disappointed that the transition did not occur, more surprised and puzzled. We began to look at ourselves very carefully. Not finding anything missing, we had to look elsewhere. That was when we began to explore outside our own dimension. It seemed that the means to do that exploring was there when we were ready to use it.

The first dimension we encountered (unlike railroad tracks, there are many parallel dimensions) was one very much like our own. This world, Elesium, was very close to the point we had just passed and seemed to be on the verge on moving out of physical reality into one that was moving much faster. We could see this new reality coming very close to theirs. As the two seemed about to merge (this was over a period of about 25 years in your time) they simply did not merge. The higher dimension faded away, became brighter and it moved to a another higher level yet, leaving the other behind. The beings in Elesium experienced an apparent increase in density and for them there seemed to be less Light. From our point of view, as observers not directly involved in the experienced, things remained the same.

At about the same time we also encountered a parallel world which was very chaotic, warlike, and somewhat disconnected from the harmonious flow of creation, much more so than yours. They appeared to be on the verge of destroying themselves and their planet. We call them Rushack. They had developed the use of solar power, channeled that knowledge into making weapons of destruction and were using these weapons against each other and against invaders from outside their solar system. As the Elesians missed their opportunity to leave physical existence, the aliens suddenly abandoned their attack on Rushack, and a truce was worked out on that world. They have been progressing very rapidly since that time. Wars have gradually, become smaller and rarer, a movement toward planet-wide cooperation has begun to grow, and peace within individuals of this world is becoming easier to find. They have still much to learn about working together, but they are now trying. They have given themselves the opportunity to begin to recognize the force outside themselves which we call the Creator. Their world is still too chaotic for us to be able to interact with them at a physical level, but we are continuing to watch them.

This apparent conjunction of events on our world and Rushack and Elesium interested us very much and we began to discover ties between them. It appeared that we had all begun at a similar and possibly identical point. At some time, separation occurred and the parallel movement began. The Rushack had separated earliest and time had moved more slowly there so they did not progress very fast. They seemed to be exploring love by completely separating themselves from it to view it from outside themselves. That separation is not possible ultimately except in the mind of the one who creates it. Their desire to maintain that separation conflicted with the naturally cohesive, uniting nature of love itself and created conflict within themselves and within their world. As they approached their imminent annihilation, it seemed that there was an inpouring of love from another level which erased some of the conflict, and more harmony was the result.

We recorded this event with a device which allows us to view it on many levels, from the physical to more etheric and spiritual levels. We can replay it as often as we wish and have studied it extensively, individually and as a group. We found at the sixth-dimensional level an outpouring of energy from our world and that of the Elesians which began at the point where our movement to the higher dimension eluded us. The energy flowed into Rushack at the point where they in turn eluded their destruction. The events were not simultaneous from our time perspective, but the energy arrived at the crucial point. They received energy from other sources, some of which we have identified and some of which we have not. One outpouring came from your world just after the end of Atlantis. Apparently your world could not accept all of what was available to it at that time and some was lost, ready to be swept into the flow of energy to Rushack.

We contemplated this set of discoveries for a very long time, putting much of our group energy into finding some meaning in it. At first we naturally thought that somehow this world had held us back from our proper goal, or that we had somehow forfeited our evolutionary position through a decision made at a higher spiritual level to give some of our forward movement to them. We have gradually come to realize that we did not really lose anything. We have increased our creative base through our explorations of parallel existence. What seemed to be a lid clamped over our progress turned out to be an opportunity to expand our knowledge of physical existence beyond anything we had learned before. We discovered we were not through with physical existence as we had thought. Our opportunity to remain within it has become an exploration into the Light potential of physical matter itself. We no longer desire to release our connection with it, but desire to learn more and more about it. We no longer feel limited by it but see it as a means of expanding ourselves and our power. Well, at least we are coming to see that more and more.

Time has become a tool rather than a barrier as we learn to see through it to the truth behind its structure. Space has become a chance to learn, rather than a limit placed in our awareness. Our bodies have become an integration point for our souls' expanding creative power. We become more and more aware of that creative power as we learn to use it at the physical level. It is not always easy. Even with a complete merging of soul consciousness into physical consciousness, which many of our race have accomplished, it is difficult to apply soul knowledge at the physical level. The creative rules which apply at the fifth- or sixth-dimensional levels are not the same as those at the third. They can be adapted and applied there, but the actual method used must be worked out by trial and error in physicality. Sometimes we do gain some insight into perfecting the process from outside our world. We have shortened the time needed to solve some problems through sharing with these new friends.

As we have expanded our consciousness into other dimensions we have grown in our creative ability to manipulate physical matter according to our will. We see that that ability is just as sacred at the physical level as at the higher levels of awareness. Those beings who serve as creators at more cosmic levels need the input of those who are focused into physical levels in order to guide them accurately, according to the Plan. We are learning to be aware of this exchange among the various levels of creation and hope to be able to serve as a bridge among them. We are finding physical existence less and less limiting and more and more we are able to use it to express our creativity spiritually.

We consider our explorations of parallel dimensions to be an exploration of our creative abilities. As we explore other dimensions we are discovering their reason for existing. I don't mean just the ability to create different forms because of slight shifts in the energy flow of conscious awareness. I mean the expansion of love through our ability to understand and flow with it. You will notice, please, I did not say our ability to use it. One cannot use love for one's own purposes without distorting the flow into disharmony and creating chaos. One must learn to see the flow, understand it, and then apply what is learned through it.

Ideally, this would involve being able to understand love and the Divine Plan from every possible perspective within the universe. Yet no one can do that unless he or she had viewed that perspective from within and without. So it is not possible to know how to work with love in a new situation unless one has already experienced it. A certain amount of trial and error is necessary and mistakes will be made until a broad enough perspective can be gained to understand the flow of love more completely. When you have an experience like Earth where each experience is very new and much that is unknown is being explored, there will inevitably be many mistakes.

The best thing about mistakes is that you can erase them. Nothing is permanent. You choose what you want to keep as part of your reality. You create your existence with your beliefs about yourself and your environment. If something in your life is not acceptable to you it will change when you realize that that is not how you want to experience life. A mistake is a part of the experiment that doesn't work. To change it, you choose to experience something. It is as simple as that. The problem is that your emotional body tends to want to continue the momentum of the experience and refuses to release it. It has trouble making the leap to the next experiment because of fear that that will not work either, or that it will miss the moment of transition.

Yet every moment is an entirely new creation. You are constantly moving in consciousness from awareness of all potential to awareness of specific focus and back to a cosmic perspective. Your physical consciousness cannot grasp infinity so it believes that it is not part of it. Your intuition is what connects you into infinity and your use of your intuition will allow you to be more aware that you do indeed exist within pure unlimitedness. That is the key to moving through other dimensions than your own. When you can accept that your way of doing things, your style of existence, your particular form are not the only possible ones, you will be able to grasp the other perspectives that are available to you.

You will also be able to create whatever you want within any dimension. You begin with your own. When that is perfected, you can begin to create or recreate others. You can maintain a base in your "home" dimension and create from there. When you are ready, you can release that and use as much as you are able of the perspective of infinity as your creative base. We are in the process of releasing our present creative base and moving to a more cosmic one. We are sure of that through the intuitive knowledge of our group consciousness. Yet we have been encouraged by some directive outside our immediate knowledge to explore laterally rather than vertically, to explore parallel dimensions rather than higher ones. Through this, we are learning much about our own creative base that we did not know before. Our ability to manipulate our own environment has increased through our observations of other dimensions. Our understanding of the flow is deeper than we ever thought possible. We now have an ability to manipulate physical matter that would have been forfeited if we had not remained at the physical, third-dimensional level.

We are also learning more about the Divine Plan by this study of alternate dimensions. We are putting together a picture of it from very specific, detailed viewpoints. As we compare the flow of other dimensions with our own, we discover a wealth of new reasons for the existence of each. For instance, we feel very strong in our ability to use love in all circumstances without having to break it down into specific aspects. It has produced much harmony and unity between ourselves. Yet we do see the advantage of your way which fractured it into many pieces. Neither way produced an instant understanding of love, but each added to an understanding of what it is and how to move with it.

We do not see that it is necessary to repeat your mistakes to gain from your experience. We can study the flow of the Divine Plan through your Earth history and learn from that. We can also share your use of love through your emotions and learn more about how to flow with the Plan. We would like to be able to share with you our way of flowing with the plan, because we feel you would be benefited by it. And we would gain from your ability to use love in so many ways.

For instance, we can create beauty here but we have not learned to bring it to the physical level as art, architecture, gardens, or fashion. We are amazed by the variety of things you can create. We never thought of doing them because we do not value physical things as you do. Your emphasis on material things has allow you to create at the physical level in a way we had not conceived of. We have very few material things. Since we learned to control the climate of our planet, we no longer need shelter, so we stopped creating it. We do maintain a space where we can gather in large number to be together because we enjoy that. We have no need for our own individual space because we can simply set ourselves apart from others, if necessary, by focusing inward.

We have observed that your need for solitude results from insecurity about your safety in groups. As you each pursue such individual aims, you lack understanding of others' needs and cannot support them. Your belief that they will inhibit the flow of your life brings you much suffering from others. We do not need things to support ourselves and prove that we are secure, because we are always secure with each other. It was not always like that, I admit. Before we agreed on a group understanding of the divine Flow, as we could experience it, there was much chaos. As we learned to share our knowledge with each other, we each expanded our understanding, harmony grew and balance was attained. This balance is not maintained at the expense of anyone's freedom to explore his or her own creative power. It is maintained by a structure that allows each to explore it with the support of the group. As I said before, there have been some who felt they had to leave the group to move in their own way, but even now we are retracing their steps to learn from their experiences.

We have learned to heal ourselves and there is no sickness or aging here. In fact, that ability was what led us to believe that we had completed our time in physical existence. Now we find that there is much healing to be done in dimensions parallel to our own and that we can never be free of potential physical harm while others are still creating death by failure to maintain healthy life. We find that we can effect healing on your planet if you will allow it, not only for individuals, but for your race. We can help you create a physical form that will be able to support itself on higher energies and within a faster flow. This also requires acceptance from you. We have that from you at nonphysical levels of awareness, but few have allowed it at the level of physical consciousness.

There are many races from many planets and dimensions which are capable of existing within the more radioactive format and higher vibrational rates of the energy field your planet is moving into. We are only one group who is involved in combining the genetic structure of these races with yours to produce a new form which will be more flexible in adapting to new energies. Some of them, like us, also need the strength of your present form to remain at the physical level. This merging and recombining of genetic structure is producing a pool of available life forms that have greater potential for continuing to exist than they do now. Some do not work at all, some not very well. We can discover which are best only by experimentation and pooling our available knowledge about such forms. We are getting much better at predicting which forms will be most successful. Your Earthly genetic structure is quite valuable for producing qualities of strength and flexibility. While you seem to lack flexibility in acceptance of those different from yourselves, your experiences with many aspects of the universal flow have made you able to deal with wide variations of energy. Most of what you lack is the ability to see beyond what you know consciously about yourselves to what you are potentially. This limit exists in your genetic structure as well as in your mind and emotions.

I know, this idea of experimenting with your bodies seems horrifying to you. It sounds as if we are creating monsters like some diabolical scientist who has no respect for life nor love of those with whom he works. This perspective is born out of your belief that the physical body is the most important thing about you. In reality, your consciousness, your immortal soul, your self as part of the divine Creator are what are important. Your physical body is only a means of existing at the physical level so you can learn from the opportunities available there. The Divine Creator does not seem to make distinctions that say one life form is more beautiful than another. Each exists to serve a specific purpose which serves all of creation and when that purpose is fulfilled the form dies or ceases to reproduce itself.

We are not limited, like you, in what kind of physical forms we can love. Perhaps it is our ability to maintain love as a unified flow which allows us to love all forms and see the beauty and potential in each. Our explorations of other dimensions have certainly added to our appreciation of what can be gained within each. We love each being born to us, no matter how unusual it might be. We give it all the love and nurturing we can and support that life to the extent that it wishes to be. Every soul born into any body has agreed to support whatever level of experimenting is available, whether it be in using love vs. hate, beauty vs. the unusual, or alternate life forms. No being is cast out of our hearts because it is different from us.

We do not see that experimentation with form is any worse than or better than experimenting with love, political or social structures, degrees of physical wealth, energy flows or anything else possible in this universe of infinite possibilities. We do see that the physical level of experiencing has great value to us as we explore our infinite creative potential. We do see that it will be a good thing to have physical bodies available in the future and that something must be done now to save them. We are able to adapt our bodies to changing energy levels because of certain genetic capabilities within them. We know how to share this genetic structure with you. It will not even produce drastic changes in your present structure, but your horror of accepting any other form in yourselves or others is limiting our ability to work with you consciously.

We have been forced to conduct our research and race-building outside your consciousness. This means you do not have the opportunity to share the learning and knowledge from the process. It is creating a gap in your movement to the next level of awareness. It also creates a gap within yourselves that prevents moving your physical bodies to that level. There is a subconscious barrier that keeps out significant changes in your bodies that would allow them to move with continuity to this new energy level. You will not be able to experience the coming changes in your present physical bodies. You will have to die and resume your physical-plane experiencing in a new body which has been brought from "outside" Earth. You will miss some of the knowledge you might gain about making this transition and will be less able to help others when you have moved to higher levels of experiencing.

Part of the link between physicality and universal Light will be lost. Establishing that link is a very important part of the divine purpose of most of you who will be reading this. You have been working very hard to bring knowledge of Light into your physical consciousness. You have worked for eons to learn more about using love while in a physical body. You must integrate the Light at the physical level to accomplish your goal. You already understand all there is to know about Light and love at your cosmic levels of consciousness. You must integrate the spiritual perspective into the physical one now. Your higher self integrates the physical into the spiritual as you do so. One cannot happen without the other. There will be a gap in your understanding of the flow if you cannot make this present transition at the physical level. Then you will probably decide to come back and try it again as you have done so many times already.

We are here to help you understand how to fulfill your purpose as we explore ours. We are not serving some macabre, deviant purpose by experimenting with your physical forms and exploring their possibilities. We are seeking new ways to allow life to continue throughout the universe. You already have the results of many past experiments with your forms on your planet as different races. Each one has its particular strength, physical as well as psychic and spiritual. You already have the opportunity available to begin to learn to love and accept others different from you.

Life did not originate on Earth. It was placed there by your Creator in the form of others who were able to assist the process of establishing a viable form there. You do not exist alone in the universe, are not left to struggle against impossible odds without any support from that universe. Allow us to be your friends and share our knowledge of life and living with you. We want to help. We will not gain from our work with you unless we can learn to blend our creative potential with yours for the greater good of both. We will not do anything you are not ready to accept. We will continue to work, as we do now, at the level where you have asked for and accepted our help. When you are ready to work consciously with us in a harmonious, completely accepting way, we will be happy to be available at the physical level. We are looking forward to that time now. We have great love for you.

Ranoash of Ataien

6

I would like to talk now about genetics, but first I must discuss what the Divine Plan is because your genetic structure depends on that. Just as each of you is a replica in miniature of Source, so the path of evolution which each of you follows is a replica of the Divine Plan. Source, from our perspective, is infinitely large and that makes each of us unbelievably small in relation to the Source, our Creator.

We each have the potential to grow back into Source again. That is our divine Potential. Yet, being such a small piece of Source we cannot express clearly what It is. The hologram is the best analogy there is. It is a pattern of Light captured on some kind of recording material. As used by physicists on Earth that material is a photographic plate. For you, as part of Source, the medium is physical existence, particularly Earth or Earth substance. Now, as you may know, you can cut up a hologram into as many pieces as you want and each piece is capable of recreating the whole picture. But as the pieces become smaller, the picture loses definition. It gets fuzzy. There is no way to regain the clarity of the whole without putting the picture back together again.

There is no perfect analogy and this is where we must leave this one. You do not have to remain a very small, fuzzy replica of Source. You can evolve within the context of this material on which you have been "pictured" or "recorded." You are alive and can grow into a new, complete, full-sized Source, yourself. And — this is what is exciting — you will become a unique, new Source, rather than an exact replica of the original one. The original "holographic replica" that you are is small, but it contains a unique combination of Source energy particles or Source aspects. Source is infinitely diversified and creative within Itself. It sees Itself in an infinite number of ways, so it divides Itself into many uniquely different parts which still potentially partake of all the qualities of the whole. You could say that Source sees Itself as each of you, complete as an individual, yet only part of the whole. It is this uniqueness which gives you your own free will. Your will is a result of what you are, therefore unlike anyone else's.

You will not follow the same path as another because your desire leads you on your own unique path. This means you each have unique experiences which shape your learning and evolution. Eventually you do rejoin the rest of the "pieces of Source" and the whole becomes One again, just as it was before but now greater because of the combination of new viewpoints and understanding that have become part of it. Source will then see a sharper image of Itself because of this splitting up and rejoining. It will have experienced learning about Itself through the many viewpoints. The hologram can never become more that it was originally. If you cut it up and put it back together again it would actually get worn out because of energy lost and would thus lose clarity. But Source gains energy, expands and grows as a result of this process. You never lose anything by separating from Source in order to explore your own viewpoint. You have the potential for gaining everything there is, and more, as you eventually become Source. You create the "more" yourself.

Is this new Source that you become separate from the original One? No, because Source by definition is everything that is. It is the complete expression of creation. We could say much more about Source and how it moves within Itself in order to explore Its creative possibilities, but this is enough for now. It will be a long, long time before you are ready to use knowledge about the cycles of Source experience in a practical way. But I do want you to understand exactly what you are. You have infinite potential within you. Your understanding of what you are grows with every step of your evolution and your ability to create increases with every bit of knowledge you integrate into your life at any level. Right now you are concerned with learning to use Source's Plan at the physical level.

As an original part of Source, you had a part in planning this creative experience — from the universe down to your physical life on Earth. Of course, those with the most experience were responsible for the greater share of shaping the experience, but if each one is to learn from that experience, each one must contribute to its shape. No one is required to participate against his or her will. There are compromises, yes, and Source Itself has the final word over that of an individual, but while you are at Source level you realize that in the infinite time available there will always be a chance for you do do exactly what you want.

So Source or some aspect of Source (it's all the same thing) decides on a plan for each creation. It is usually a group plan, especially within this Source (or Source as we are now experiencing It). Many plans are presented by individuals or groups, discussed, and studied before the final one is approved. Often small "trial runs" are made to check out details if the creative experience is to be a large one, such as this one. Some of these trials are never terminated and play out their destinies at the same time as the larger one. These can serve as alternate realities which reinforce the larger, more complicated one. If they reach a successful conclusion they provide a powerful surge of energy at the time of their completion which gives a thrust to the other, similar creative experiences which are running on similar frequencies. If they develop snags in their movement back to Source, they serve as warnings of what is ahead for the others. Not all these problems show up in the trial runs. Sometimes the larger experience magnifies the defects within the prototype, making them more obvious and easier to interpret. Several of these "trials," for Earth specifically, were successfully completed at the time of your Harmonic Convergence, adding to the positive forward movement of evolution for Earth.

When enough has been learned about the Plan being decided on, the actual building of its structure begins. The only energy available to use in building is love. That is what Source is: love and nothing else, pure, simple, unconditional love. When this love is focused through the consciousness of individuals into a specific plan it becomes Light. The original blueprint for creation is a Light framework on which the building begins. Since this plan is limited to specific goals it is no longer complete Source, but still partakes of Source's potentialities because it is formed of aspects of Source. As more details are added into the original framework it becomes richer in its complexity and more diversified in its viewpoints. As it becomes more detailed and focused it can appear to those involved in it to be further from Source.

The structure is maintained by the thoughts of those working with it. Thought is the framework which the Light follows or illuminates. When the thoughts of those who are maintaining this structure cease or turn from the creative framework, it ceases to exist. Its energy goes elsewhere. At the end of every creative experience, Source's thoughts turn inward, the energy in drawn back into the Oneness and nothing exists any longer, until Source has a new idea to pursue.

The more detailed or specific the part of the structure any being is involved in studying, exploring, or extending, the more separated within Source it tends to feel. So a sort of hierarchy of support for focusing the structure is arranged. Those with the most experience and ability in creating work with the big picture, concentrating on the flow of the whole pattern. Others are responsible for working at the various levels from very comprehensive to very detailed. This allows a sort of gradation of "separation" so that there is always someone close by who does not feel quite as disconnected from Source as the one on the next level of complexity.

This hierarchy is arranged first on universal orders. This part of the structure of the Plan is understood and explored by twelve beings, usually known as the Council of Twelve, who are the highest level of creation apart from Source Itself. Their thoughts form the structure of this universe and focus the general flow patterns of its evolution and movements. These twelve beings have perfected their creative abilities through working in many levels of previous plans and try to understand as much as they can the absolute will of Source. That will is the original purpose decided on by the whole, all those working within it. They serve as the ultimate link back into the Source consciousness. They help you hold on to your Source connection by their knowing that you are part of Source and never separate from it. Part of their thought projection which forms creation involves knowing that it is all Source and there is nothing in it that is not Source.

The next major level in the structure of the Plan is the galactic one. There is another council, twelve again, for this galaxy, which operates within the universal framework to bring that structure into the next level. They maintain the connection that makes sure the galactic plan carries out the intent of Source as it comes from the universal level. They are concerned with coordinating the activities of a group of stars and planetary systems. As this solar system has learned to carry out its specific purposes, it has been able to understand more clearly what is going on at this level. It has learned to work with the twelve beings who are focusing it and to understand how the structure is supposed to work. At first the beings at the solar system level were concentrating very hard on learning to run it. As they became more comfortable with what they were doing, they were able to "look up from their work" and communicate more easily with their teachers at the galactic level.

This same thing is happening at Earth level now. Some of you finally understand enough about making life on Earth work to begin to enjoy some of the beautiful divine connections available beyond physical existence. Your bodies can run themselves with the help of your subconscious and you don't have to think constantly about keeping your heart beating or your hormones balanced. It's not that you stop thinking about them, but that the process has become automatic, a part of whatever you are doing and that you do without conscious effort. Your subconscious mind takes over the task of thinking about running your body and your conscious mind can then think about creating new things or variations on the old. (Some mistakes have crept into your subconscious "programming" and everything doesn't always function perfectly, but the absurdity and uselessness of these patterns give you an opportunity to correct them with conscious input.)

You have learned to stretch your minds to new levels beyond Earth and are beginning to understand more about yourselves as cosmic consciousness. You are eager to learn more about what lies beyond your immediate realm of experience. You are learning to understand increasingly complex structure through your mastery of physical things and your ability to create them. Unfortunately, your emotional development hasn't always kept pace with your mental development. As a race, you don't always have the ethical and spiritual experience to use your knowledge well. The minority of you who do have that individually do not know how to work with it as a group which can focus a planet-wide ethic based on spiritual knowledge, which can direct the activities of Earth. That is what you are working on now. You are learning to understand more of what the whole Plan requires and to work as a group to focus it for Earth.

Your planetary hierarchy is the next level of the structure of the Plan and the one that serves as your immediate guidance system. It consists of many beings who have experienced physical life on Earth and have learned to balance all aspects of themselves within that experience to the point where they understand how it coordinates with the larger plan and how to implement that plan at the physical level. They are your most familiar and, often, most loved teachers and guides. They sometimes seemed like gods to you, but you are learning that there are "gods" greater than they are with whom you can communicate. They are encouraging you and helping to introduce you to this broader perspective because, in the end, in order for physical existence to be perfect, those at the physical level must be the ones who administer and control it.

You have much to learn, right? You must begin with yourselves to perfect the operation of your life so it can be free of disease and in balance with all levels of self. You must learn to live in a way that supports others, as well as yourselves, and the Earth itself. You must be balanced and clear in your emotions so they do not distort your understanding. You must learn to communicate with each other so you are aware of others' needs as well as your own, because you only seem to be an individual, alone. You are part of everything around you and imbalance anywhere can affect your own balance. If abundance, for instance, is not distributed equally, you must always fear that someone will take what is yours. When self-esteem and survival depend on physical possessions, you must fear their loss. Fear blocks love. It also blocks clear communication.

To continue with the structure of the Plan, the thoughts of those who are focusing it serve as the structure which is precipitated as Light into the next lower level of existence. It takes the shape of an icosahedron, a geometric figure which has twelve corners, or vertices, and twenty faces. The Council of Twelve for Earth serves as the corners, and as they focus their thoughts together, the streams of their consciousness interlace to form a system of geometric figures within it which are the other levels of the Plan. Your planetary logos, Sanat Kumara, is the most visible member of this council.

A dodecahedron (twelve faces) is generated within the larger figure and another icosahedron is formed within the dodecahedron. This process goes on forever, if you so choose. These two figures interact to form an octahedron with eight triangular faces. Another symmetrical figure can be constructed on each face consisting of six triangles, to form a tetrahedron, which you know as a double-ended, three-sided pyramid. When you look at this double pyramid through evolution as time, it becomes a spiraling tower of pyramids into which fits, very nicely, a structure very important to your physical existence, a molecule of DNA. Your genetic material is essentially Light precipitated through the structure of the Plan into a system of evolution. All DNA fits within the spiraling pyramids of the moving tetrahedron. Individual differences are due to the variation of the thoughts projecting the Light flow within them. I give you this not to frustrate you with impossible mental pictures, but to begin to show you the symmetry and harmony of the whole. The actual picture is naturally much more complex, but the basic numbers here can be important keys in understanding yourselves and your universe. Three, six, twelve, four and twenty are important building blocks for creation.

Your own Light structure resembles that of the universe as does that of every other conscious entity within it — galaxies, stars, planets, even continents, mountains and lakes, as well as animals and plants. The pyramidal structure of DNA is focused within the geometric structures of the universe and itself becomes a point which can be extended or enlarged into enveloping figures. It is a potential focus for evolution. Each DNA molecule projects around itself a dodecahedron which projects, in turn, an icosahedron. Each atom of physical matter has its own consciousness — primitive, yes, but with infinite potential. Each atom has its own Light structure of crystalline geometrics, fitting into the perfect symmetry of the universe. These geometrics are multidimensional and multilevel, so are impossible to imagine with your third-dimensional mind. Our geometric picture is very limited as it is extremely difficult to describe in words the very complex, multilayered, multidimensional geometry of the universe.

There are certain groups within the Plan who work specifically with DNA itself and subgroups who work with its permutations. Each variation is designed to support physical existence in a special way, but each is built on the same basic pyramidal pattern, which is basic to the universe, galaxy or planet. These beings who are working with DNA at the spiritual level begin to organize it into a system which fits into the seemingly infinite geometrics of the whole. As the consciousness of each of you focuses more deeply into physical existence, you gradually take from the whole what you need to create your own physical body. If you are on Earth, you have gathered the atoms and DNA prototypes that have been specifically designed to be most useful to your specific purpose on Earth.

When your physical bodies are complete, they become a multidimensional pattern of Light in the geometric patterns we have been discussing. At the physical level you do not resemble a symmetrical geometric solid, partly because you are not yet complete, but also because you cannot see the whole of what you are at all levels. From more spiritual levels, you appear to be a pulsing, flowing Light field which is tending more and more toward the shape of a perfect twelve-sided figure, the dodecahedron, at the sixth-dimensional level. At the twelfth-dimensional level you resemble the twenty-sided figure, the icosahedron. Your physical body is a small pattern of double pyramids, the tetrahedron, within the larger figure. It fits precisely into its own little corner of the immensely larger pattern of Light.

The energy in your DNA flows from one molecule to the next, moving at a rate consistent with your spiritual awareness. It also flows into and through the interlocking, contiguous patterns of everything around you. Once the energy has been used by you and "imprinted" through that use by the DNA, it has an affinity for other DNA with similar imprinting from any dimension. It is easier to use as the flow that energizes other DNA. It is the appropriate material to use for repairing and restructuring other DNA. There is little actual difference in DNA structure among life forms on Earth. Minor variations make you different from apes or dolphins. Since our world is a parallel to yours and comes from the same origin, our DNA structure varies from yours about as much. The variation exists because of the nature of the physical matter itself which is being organized by the DNA. Your Earth has purposes slightly different from ours which have literally shaped physical matter itself. Your Earth is more complex so your DNA has slight variations which allow you to use your available physical substances to their best advantage. If you came to live on our planet, you would come to look like us because your DNA would begin to adapt to the available material for building cells, not because your essential self-consciousness changed or because we altered you in some way.

In giving you the bigger picture, I hope to convey the very minute differences between us and the great similarities. It is your cosmic intent which ideally shapes your form, not the influence of other systems of life. Your divine connection to Earth, as a part of its life flow, determines the subtle variations between your form and that of beings from other worlds. All life is compatible within the harmony and balance of the whole. Interaction between life forms is part of the evolutionary progress of the whole.

We use our own DNA to heal your physical bodies because it is readily available and can serve as the ideal pattern for yours, with very minor variations. The important point about our DNA structure, and yours, is that it is designed to support evolving consciousness. The pattern for expanding consciousness through learning and experiencing is important and determines the form. DNA is intended to be flexible and able to flow with the changing intentions of the whole as well as you own. Your emphasis on the importance of the form itself has created some errors in your DNA structure which allow disease and aging. It literally created a change in your DNA structure which blocks the normal evolution of your DNA. So it is blocking expansion of consciousness and understanding of yourselves as cosmic rather than physical beings. It also creates disease and its energy runs down, causing aging. It eventually gets too far out of alignment with the creative flow to be supported by it and your body dies.

Our DNA is free of these errors and we have been trying to share some of it with you so that you can use it as as pattern on which to restructure your own DNA. This is working at unconscious, more spiritual levels where you are not limited in your understanding of the ideal structure of your physical bodies. At the physical level, there is too much fear of being turned into something monstrous for you to consciously allow this help. Fear of what we are doing to you is blocking clear communication of our intent and certainly of our love.

Once you have gained understanding of the life form you are using, it is time to explore the meaning of other forms. The universe does not stand still. It moves constantly and that movement is always constructive and progressive. By holding on to one stage of evolution you stop the flow into your system and lose contact with the rest of creation. Since only part of you is holding on to this misperception that your physical bodies are the ultimate, perfected result of your evolution, the flow has stopped only partially. This part is out of balance with the part that is moving and has created disharmonies which are causing disease and inability to adjust to the new energies. We are trying to interject some corrective factors at the physical level which will restore balanced movement.

I do not mean to say that you are not the Creator's crowning achievement or that your form is not adapted to perfect expression of your consciousness as divine beings. It is your consciousness that is the important, evolving part of you. Your creative abilities are the ultimate product of your evolution. You are created in the image of your Creator but you are not yet complete until you become It and can create as It does, with unlimited love. Only in this sense are you not yet complete in your purpose, because you are always perfect in the eyes of the Creator. So is every other life form in the universe.

The shape of your physical form is determined at the galactic level. Those who coordinate creation from that level (sixth-dimensional and above) focus the patterns of Light which flow through those interlocking geometric structures into your bodies. That Light is the energy which supports your physical structure, shapes it, and leads it forward along its evolutionary path. When one level of development is complete, the Light begins to emphasize the structure of the next level, molding your bodies, gradually, into the shape required for the coming, new level. If you can connect consciously into these changing patterns of Light and make them a part of your body you will make each transition without difficulty. If your consciousness is stuck somewhere and you cannot connect with the new vision and flow with it, you require help to maintain your place within the structure of the whole, which is constantly changing.

If the break in the flow of the ideal occurs at a very spiritual level, the corrections can be made there. Since your discontinuity in flow occurs between the fifth and fourth, then the fourth- and third-dimensional levels, help must come into those levels. We have worked with you a great deal at the fourth-dimensional level, as some of you with the ability to retain conscious awareness of your astral experiences know. If you can flow energy from that level consciously into the physical you can then begin to facilitate the necessary changes. If you are blocked in moving between the third- and fourth-dimensional levels, help must come into the physical dimension itself, with your permission at some level of consciousness, of course.

A well-balanced emotional body which can work well with your mental part is necessary to bring the energizing, healing Light flow into your physical body. You must have love for your physical body, or at least some desire to connect with it as Light. Love activates the flow, making it easier, promoting the alignment with the ideal, and drawing your physical cells and DNA into the ideal flow pattern. A balanced, healthy emotional body is the mechanism for the connection of your body into the healing, transformational flow of the new energies. A balanced, open mind can grasp the changing patterns of Light which channel the flow to you. A clear spiritual connection to your soul gives you the guidance you need in finding the appropriate pattern within the Divine Plan which supports your spiritual purpose.

Some of your inability to change comes from the atomic material from which your bodies are constructed. Earth, itself, is stuck in its inability to move forward. We will discuss that later. Since your DNA is also composed of this physical material, it is difficult for you to change it. We have been helping you to prepare, at levels slightly more subtle than the physical, to begin to work on this at a planet-wide, physical level. When that is completed to the necessary degree, we will begin to work more directly on the physical level to promote the changes.

As I said, our DNA represents the ideal pattern and the energy we use to maintain our own physical structures can be used to heal and transform yours. The work we are doing with you will eventually involve injections of our own genetic material into your physical bodies. You could call it an "unlimited life" genetic factor, which can be integrated into your DNA structure and used by your cells to perfect and evolve your physical form and increase its energy potential to a level that is more aligned with the increasing energy levels. This requires us to make some physical contact with Earth, probably with some individuals who are able to begin to share our help with you. It will be difficult for us to make extensive contact with humanity for some time. Some of you are already beginning to allow us to work directly with your physical bodies, but the conscious permission is not yet balanced with all levels of your sometimes very confused selves and we are having very limited success. If you reject what we offer at any level of consciousness or subconsciousness, it becomes useless to you, or, worse yet, poison. Remember, your mind controls your reality. If you think you are being manipulated by an alien plot to steal your genetic material or enslave you, you will create just such a situation.

Ranoash of Ataien

If you are able to accept, at all levels of self, that the Divine Plan is bringing you everything you need to maintain your alignment into it, then you can allow your bodies to be transformed and healed. If you can trust us and allow us to use our love to guide our working together, we can begin to approach you in a way that will be more satisfactory for the purposes of all. We have followed your evolution for a long time. We are full of love and admiration for what you have already done and what you will do. We can see some of the creative possibilities opening for you now, and we want to help you make the most of them. To do so, you must be able to remain in physical bodies on your Earth. We want to help you create bodies that are healthy, radiant with joy and love, and capable of transforming physical existence into a level which is in complete harmony with the whole of creation.

Ranoash of Ataien

7

We looked at the process of creation from several points of view in the last chapter. I mentioned that sometimes small, experimental prototypes of a specific creative experience were set up. My planet was one of those. We were all experienced in the specific aspects of creativity which were being used in this current universe. It was to be used to explore previously unused portions of Source energy. Source is composed of infinite amounts of energy, basically love, and there are infinite ways of using it. If this were not so, Source would have limitations. Limitation within Source would cause it to eventually "run down" and die and that never happens.

Source everlastingly continues to explore Itself. It integrates what It knows about Itself with what It is exploring. The pattern of each creation is built from what is known and understood by its various aspects — us, as individuals — so we can explore what is not yet known or has not yet been explored by us. What we know, of course, can support us. It is what we know how to use. We know how the known will react to our creative impulses and that gives us the courage to move into it eagerly and confidently. It holds no surprises because it is part of ourselves which we understand very well. We can take as much of it into ourselves as we choose and everything will fit into place.

The unknown is just that, and more so. It is unknown to everything except undifferentiated Source. When Source fragments into separate aspects, the known and the unknown seem to separate from each other and the challenge of creation begins. Every creation presents a new set of unknown aspects which must be integrated before Source can become whole again in the conscious sense. What we understand becomes good or positive to our consciousness. What cannot be integrated into our conscious system of knowledge becomes something negative. You call it evil.

This negative substance from Source acts like a magnet on our understanding. It draws us into it, seemingly against our better judgment. Since we know nothing about it we have no choice except to begin to experiment. Our first experiment gives us a conscious connection into it. We begin to understand something about it, even if it is just that what we tried does not work. We must try something else and so we are drawn more and more into this unknown negative. Our postulations and plans seem to be a web that entangles us more and more into this negativity. It is part of ourselves, really, since we are Source exploring Itself.

We do have the Divine Plan to guide us, which was set up from a point of wholeness within Source. The most important thing that we know there is that Source is love and that we are Source. No matter how we look at ourselves, how much we fracture ourselves, how specifically we look at different parts of ourselves, that will never change. We can refuse to recognize that and refuse to move with the flow of the Divine Plan, but that course, carried to its final end, leads to loss of consciousness, because we begin with that ultimate knowledge that we are Source. Ultimately, consciousness is knowing we are Source, so denial of that means loss of consciousness and oblivion. That would make us part of what is unknown, still part of Source, but not part of the creative experience.

We said that the Plan was "held in place" by those aspects of Source who understand creating the best. Some of them also serve as part of the prototype experiences. They can make a sort of quick run-through of the whole Plan, scanning the elements of its purpose and seeing how the unknown parts of it will affect it. They have had a great deal of experience in guiding others in previous creations and have a great deal of knowledge about how the unknown affects different situations and individuals. We on our world were part of a prototype experience that was to explore this Divine Plan, especially to see how it would affect the part of Source which would become Earth. The conscious entity which was to become Earth had chosen to incorporate into itself a great deal more than usual of the negative, unexplored substance.

Our teachers tell us that Earth's love for Source was so great that it desired to serve Source by learning as much as it could. It wanted to help Source expand though the knowledge it could gain about Itself as Source. It was very aware that that meant it was exploring love, because that is what Source is. Earth was cautioned that love was very powerful and that when not understood could swallow up conscious-ness and cause one to become lost in its infinite unknown. But Earth was so full of love that it was sure it could integrate anything it needed to learn about unknown Source and make it part of the known power of Source.

Many were inspired by Earth's example and chose to help her in her task. They were challenged by the knowledge that they could bring so much new power into Source by exploring the unknown and making it part of their understanding. As their understanding grew, so would their conscious ability to use love, for that is all there is. The more experienced cocreator-creators within the Plan recognized the potential for this Earth experiment, but also realized its potential pitfalls. They knew that sometimes it has not been possible to inte-grate everything unknown within a creative experience into a system of knowledge about self, and the whole experience must be ended as it literally dissolves into chaos. No new knowledge is gained and Source simply picks up the pieces and takes them back into Itself.

So a number of trial runs were carried out. Some were successful, some were not. Ours was one that was. It was so successful that its life was extended, in a sense, and it was never terminated. It is still going on, always moving to its successful conclusion. Since it is already complete, we have knowledge of our ability to succeed within this Plan. We also have access to the knowledge gained by less successful experiments. Since our part in the plan was a less detailed, simpler version than yours, it does not require so much time, energy, and space. Our time would seem to run much slower than yours, but we reach the goal first. One hundred thousand of our years corresponds to one of yours. Time is relative, however, to what one wants to do. We have chosen to remain in the unfinished segment of this universe rather than experience the end which has already occurred for us.

At the beginning of this creation, when the prototypes had been evaluated and necessary corrections made in the Divine Plan for it, we experienced a sort of slow falling out of consciousness in our knowledge of ourselves. We no longer knew that we were the experts who had already completed this creation. By agreeing to allow our part to continue rather than be withdrawn into the more spiritual levels of creation, we had to give up our knowledge of our glorious conclusion. We have relearned it by going deeper into physicality. The strength we gained there has allowed us to integrate our knowledge of physical existence into our spiritual connection which was, of course, never broken. Our success had formed a bridge back to Source which was always there for us, it just took us a while to see it. When we realized that we were always making the correct choices, we knew that we had already reached the point of realignment with Source. Our new knowledge of physical existence finally had allowed us to see that it was also part of the bridge. We have not lost anything by "repeating" the experience continuously, because we have learned much more.

Our part of this creation had been a sort of survey of the problems that arose within it, as well as the potentials. We did not go as deeply as you into the details, but we have gone far enough that we, through our prior knowledge, can understand much of what you are experiencing. We can understand enough that we can offer some solutions. We will not bring them forward unless you ask us to and we are certainly not going to solve your problems for you. You must do that yourselves. You are part of Earth and must integrate the problem and the solutions into your experience as your own conscious knowledge. We can help you at any level of consciousness which is aware of us and is willing to work with us. Right now that is in the fifth dimension and higher. From that viewpoint within your consciousness you can begin to see that we are a part of the structure of the Plan and that we can work with you as part of it for your benefit. There is more understanding at the sixth-dimensional level where there is much love shared between us.

These new energies which the Earth is experiencing are a direct result of the part of the universe it is entering. It is a part of the galaxy where there are fewer boundaries between dimensions, both higher and parallel ones. It is not possible to bring the use of the boundaries set within the third dimension into this new energy field. The energy is so much more intense, the rate of its flow so much faster that there is no support for such limitations. Limitation requires a slowing down of movement, such as moving through a corridor with many doors. If you have to stop and open each door it will take much longer to move down the corridor than when the doors have been removed. This new energy field is a part of the spiral of evolution that has fewer doors. They are not all gone, you are not yet ready for that, but there is enough freedom for movement now to make you feel somewhat dizzy because of the rate at which you are moving.

You haven't yet learned to place all of this into the "reality" of your third-dimensional awareness. You don't yet have the conceptual structure available to be able to grasp it with your conscious minds. This book is an attempt to help you develop a new conceptual system which will allow you to think about these things, feel comfortable with them and use them at the physical level. There is much knowledge already available to you about higher dimensions and some of you have made good use of it. However, this knowledge has been brought through the old conceptual framework and is limited by it. You need more specific understanding about how to apply it at the physical level. I know, there have been some who have transcended their third-dimensional awareness with what is already available. They are even now providing a bridge for you to the same understanding.

But the Earth keeps changing constantly and the solutions never remain the same. What was true yesterday no longer works today. The structure that once took you to the heights of ecstasy no longer works. You must maintain a clearer connection to the Earth itself in order to remain in the flow of changing energies. You must remain flexible in your approach to that flow and allow your understanding of it to change with it. Creation never repeats anything in exactly the same way. It explores Itself by trying out variations of one theme and those variations are infinite. One solution leads to thousands, maybe millions of new areas to explore. Perfecting one level leads to an opening which creates many opportunities for new learning. And creation is vast enough in its scope to allow for all of them, if you choose.

If this overwhelms your mind, be comforted that that is one reason for some of the limitation at the physical level. You are required to only look at one set of opportunities, one problem, one part of yourself at a time there. However, when you have finished that, you must be willing to again open to the broader picture and to put the pieces back into it. You have been looking so long at small pieces of self that you have forgotten how to see the greater ones. The new energy field is literally forcing you to do so. It is tearing you out of your old habit structure and moving you into a new concept of Earth and your own identity.

On one hand, you see Earth as responsible for the limitations which you must break out of. On the other hand, you are realizing more and more that you are part of Earth. I will add that Earth and your relationship to it are the key for breaking those barriers of limitation. You will not expand yourself in the direction originally set in the Plan by leaving Earth. You will not find your creative power, your full cocreator-cocreatorship with Source, by separating from her.

Remember, we said you had come here to work with Earth to discover new ways of using love creatively. Your purpose here is predicated on hers. She not only holds the original, magnificent goal; Source gave her the means to reach it. By agreeing to work with her, your power became intertwined with hers, you literally became part of her for purposes of reaching this goal. There is more of you, yes, that is working on other goals, but they need not detract nor negate the importance of this one. All the love and Light which you have brought to Earth in whatever you have done here has been shared with the whole of what she is — animal, mineral, plant, human, and spiritual. That contribution has become a power reserve which is magnified by its mingling with the contribution of all others who are part of Earth. It is what you must accept as part of yourself and learn to use creatively now.

We said that all matter that comprises Earth has been shaped by her intention. The atoms which comprise your body have been shaped by Earth's purpose even though they remain in the flow of all of creation. The rest of creation supports their commitment and provides the energy to maintain the appropriate form for carrying out that purpose. The problems which arose within this purpose are shared by all who are part of Earth. The blocks and misunderstanding that have arisen because these difficulties in using previously "undisciplined" creative energies have become locked in the physical atoms of Earth and in your bodies. Part of your purpose here is to help release these blocks which have become part of you through your physicality.

The good news is that you know how to do this and that the new energies can remove them for you if you are willing to let them go. The bad news is that you have learned to hang on to these misperceptions and blocks as a support system which helps you make sense out of the confusion of physical existence. For instance, if the Creator is love, and there is nothing but love in the universe, why is it so hard to find and use love on Earth? Why does Earth seem to treat you with so little love? One answer is that you are using love in new ways. There were no roads using love already laid through the new areas you are exploring for Source. You are learning by trial and error how to move through those areas and find ways to use the unfamiliar energies as love. Source gave you experimentation as a method of exploring Itself. It wants to learn everything! You agreed to leave no stones unturned in your explorations and then enthusiastically chose to go even further.

But you forgot that. Love didn't work so you decided there was something wrong with your love. Earth, too, was learning how to use this raw creative power and you didn't like the way she supported you so you thought she was the jailer who lured you here and didn't fulfill her promises. She didn't seem to love you. These misperceptions allow your conscious mind to make sense out of the senselessness of the apparent lack of love. When you could no longer see love, it stopped flowing. When you couldn't see love in yourself you could no longer use it. Sometimes you died at many levels from lack of love. If you hated your bodies they became diseased and you died. If you hated what you sensed around you, your emotions died and you became incapable of feeling at all. If you could no longer see beauty and harmony, your mind could not create it and your world became dark, dirty, and miserable.

One thing was accomplished by all this. About three hundred years ago there was a meeting at the spiritual level of all beings who were part of Earth. They decided that they had gone as far as necessary into darkness and negativity and it was now time to get out. This was significant, because many times before, such meetings had resulted in the decision to go deeper into it. Now you all felt, at this higher level, you must do anything to reverse the process. You were made aware that this present energy opening was coming and would destroy everything that could not move to the new level. Immersion in negativity was no longer a valid choice for experiencing. There were still some who felt some stones should not be left unturned, but they were outvoted. It finally took two world wars to effect the clearing that was necessary to begin reversing the flow of Earth's creativity. It is not done yet, but much of the potential for complete destruction has been released.

Your ability to release old patterns from within yourselves is one great key which can preserve what is useful on Earth now and release the need to experience destructive cleansing at the physical level. As you learn to use love (as Light) as part of physical existence you are building a means for Earth to move to the next level in a smooth, effortless transition. You must let go of the old thought patterns which are creating lack of love, of abundance, of justice, of beauty, of freedom and of joy. So let's look a little more at what some of these patterns are.

One is that you are dependent on something outside yourself to bring you what you need. This misperception was begun as you lost your knowledge that you were part of Source and shared in everything that It is. When you no longer know that you have wholeness within you, you begin to create a life full of lack and limitation. You have cut off the spiritual support line which brings you everything you need. This was compounded when you began to feel you weren't part of Earth. Then Source could not support you through her, either. Source made you partners with Earth in this creative experience and gave each of you the resources you need to support each other. Earth can provide for all your needs and give you opportunities to express yourself creatively. You can give Earth the opportunity to transform herself by using what she provides with love and caring. You can also provide a means of bringing energies and ideas to her from nonphysical levels into physicality.

When you learn that all your needs are provided for within the Plan and through your alignment with it, you will no longer want for anything. When you know that your Creator loves you, you no longer need to depend on others for love. You can share your love without expectations because you already have all that you need. When you know that your power is within yourself, you won't need someone or something to give you the ability to create what you need. You will no longer need someone outside yourself who has more power than you and you will cease to create that. You will create, instead, the means of using your own power.

Look at the ways other people or things control you. Where is your life not under your own control? Don't look just for circumstances in which you depend on others for money or physical support, but look for emotional control. Who makes you angry? Who makes you feel helpless? Who can get you involved in things you don't want to do? Why do you let them do that? What would happen if you did not allow that? Ask yourself these questions and listen very carefully to all the answers that come up from inside yourself, those "random" thoughts that don't seem to follow the track you want to pursue. Write them down. Let your imagination help you come up with lots of reasons, even if they sound ridiculous. What you hear will be your subconscious telling you what is in its programming. Some of it is pretty ridiculous, but that may be just what is determining how your life goes. When you have thoroughly released the fear and conviction that this is how your life must be, you can begin to create one in which you are in control.

You may feel dependent on someone, somehow, for the money you need to live. Should this mean your money cannot come through someone else? No, money is physical energy, but still essentially thought energy. It is part of the system you have developed to flow abundance. I mean that no one should be able to control you because he or she gives you money. The money comes not from them, but through them, because you have asked for it at some level and it is your right to receive it. It is one way for the Creator to bring it to you, but not the only way. Find something you like to to, something in which you can share your creativity with others, and through that sharing you will receive what you need. But you must be free to create what you need without control by others. To be free to create clearly is to be clear within yourself of subconscious beliefs which contradict that freedom.

Will it help if you sit for hours and repeat over and over, "I am in control, I am free"? Well it might help, but if doing that means you are not also looking inside yourself to find out why you are not in control or free, it will not help much. These hidden reasons are not always easy to find, but you can learn to recognize them by studying situations in which you are not in control and not free to carry out your own creative ideas. Your life is a result of your programming, conscious and subconscious, so you have a continuous showing of what it is in every detail, one after the other. One thing the affirmation may do is stimulate your subconscious to show you why it cannot create situations where you are in control or free. It will create the opposite of your affirmation. This doesn't mean the affirmation backfired, just that your subconscious needs help in straightening out its ability to create freedom for you.

Another misperception on Earth is that it is difficult to blend male and female energies. This seems to require a complicated set of rituals to set the stage for the blending. It requires a system of control by the male side to ensure enough support for it. Each sex has specific qualities attributed to it. Men are active, in control, more important. They are the talkers and have the best ideas. Women are passive, submit easily to control, and must defer to the male when desires conflict. They are the best listeners. They don't believe that their ideas are any good.

There is a constant battle between the two for supremacy and control. These ideas do not mirror the ideal. They are the misprogramming that creates a life that is not balanced, not in control and lacking in creative power.

This occurs not only in male-female relationships. Sexual relationships have become an important way for you of Earth to work out your dynamic-receptive relationship to Source. Are you supposed to sit here, meditate a lot and let Source work Its will through you? Or are you supposed to take your destiny into your own hands and create it all by yourself? Obviously, neither answer is correct. You must balance your dynamic ability to move with your receptive ability to listen to the Plan for guidance and to those around you for cooperation, because, remember, you came here as a group. The plan you set up at other spiritual levels was to be part of the Earth and to share your creative experience. When you have learned to listen for direction from within and then to step out confidently to take responsibility for your decisions, you find that you do not need someone else to do something for you in order to accomplish what you want. When you learn to listen to how your actions affect others and adjust those actions accordingly, you will move more surely into your creative opportunities on Earth. And Earth will be able to support you because you will be open to her help.

As you learn how to be dynamic yourself without impacting another or inhibiting another's creativity, and as you learn to be receptive without letting others control you, you will become balanced within yourself. Your creative power will flow as you choose and as you need it. It will not be distorted by your own subconscious misbeliefs that it is wrong to act, or that you cannot have what you want.

There is a deep misperception on Earth that being physical makes you evil. God is more spiritual than you. Angels are more spiritual than you. It is not possible to be spiritual when you are in a physical body. It is true that you have different ways of expressing Light and love as a physical being, but those ways are not less important. It has been difficult to learn how to express your spiritual ideas on Earth, but your divine inner self has always been inside you, inspiring you to keep working on it. It is there reminding you that you are part of Source, no less than any other part, because each of you has the same potential to recreate the whole of Source.

Never mind how hard it seems. Learn to look at what you do on Earth as an exercise in creating with love. That is all there is to create with anyway. You might as well use that information consciously. You have an infinite amount of time to perfect your experiments. There are no failures, only the lack of will or courage to try again. You can choose to call what you don't understand evil. You can allow that to fill your thoughts, but remember, you are what you think. If you are looking for what you call evil you will find it and it will become part of you. As you look for love you recreate yourself in the Creator's image. It uses love to Create. It allows love to guide and support what It does not yet understand, drawing negativity into the flow of Its Plan and learning to use it creatively.

Another misperception on Earth is that death is a necessary part of life. Let's take a look at that. What death really does is allow you to start over when you have gotten completely stuck or have gone as far as you can. When you have moved the physical matter in your cells as far as you can without recognizing its connection to Source and its Light, your body gets old and dies. Then you go back to a higher level where you remember you are Light and where you can see the Light in physical matter. You get refocused, collect your Light around you, and go back again into another physical body to try again to make it Light. You forget your Light as soon as you become physical again and the Light you brought with you eventually runs out and you get old again, or get sick and die.

As you learn to connect with the part of yourself that knows it is Light, you are able to replace the original Light you brought into your physical body. The more you recognize your own Light potential the more Light can flow through you and keep your cells healthy and young. The more you search within self for places that do not recognize their Light, the more complete and consistent that flow becomes. When you have completely balanced the flow of Light within all your cells and you can allow them to use all the Light they need to be healthy, you will never be ill and you will cease to get old. Using love generates that Light. Remember, love directed as thought is Light. Loving yourself and your body allows you to direct the flow of Light into it.

Does this mean you will live forever in the same physical body? Only if you choose to. The next step is to learn to control your body so it will do anything you want it to. You will learn to change it into whatever you want it to be. You will be able to release the physical form and flow the Light into more subtle forms. Since you have the conscious knowledge of how to shape it, you will then be able to reshape that Light into whatever form you choose. Lots of beings on Earth can do that and have done that. Your mythology and spiritual literature is full of stories of what you can do and become.

Your DNA is designed to guide the formation of a body that knows how to use Light as its support structure and knows how to flow as love. This body was intended to support a consciousness that functions on many levels besides the physical one you are now aware of. This body is was intended to function as the full expression of your soul's creativity. That doesn't mean it is the only full expression of Source's creativity. Remember Source is infinite and It expresses Itself through infinite variations of Itself. Your body was designed to be one step in exploring your potential, to help you explore the potential of physical existence. To do that the program that runs it must be clear of misperceptions that you are not Light, that you cannot use Light here, and that you do not know how to use love.

Healing and rejuvenating your body cannot be done only on a physical level. It includes transforming all of your thinking processes, conscious and subconscious, into alignment with the ideal flow of the Divine Plan. It includes releasing any beliefs that distort the perfect, symmetric, balanced shape of your Light. It means recognizing that you are part of the divine Structure of the universe so that structure can support you as it was intended to.

It also means being willing to take responsibility with Source for creating this universe, this Earth and your life. No one else can do it for you. You are your own little universe. Your consciousness is what shapes it. You are Source for your cells, your organs, life around you as it affects you. Are you acting like a loving father-mother support system for your body, your experiencing? Are you willing to allow all that the universe provides to support you and love you? Do you believe there is a Divine Plan that is guiding your path to a glorious fulfillment of your purpose? Well, maybe not completely yet, but I think we are making progress here.

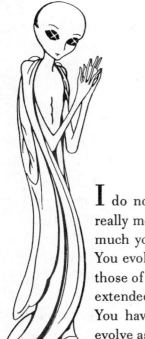

8

I do not think that many of you understand what it really means to be a part of physical existence and how much you are committed to evolving as part of Earth. You evolve as an independent conscious entity, yes, but those of you who are what you call "Lightworkers" have extended your area of responsibility beyond yourselves. You have committed yourselves to helping the Earth evolve as a part of your own evolutionary process. So let us discuss what that means.

The atom is the most elementary division of consciousness in this universe. Subatomic particles have consciousness also, but it is part of the whole, not divided. Your current explorations into the understanding of these particles and discovery of their power is one aspect of the expansion of consciousness that is going on now on Earth. They symbolize the higher energies that are available to become a part of your physical reality. The new elements created in your atomic accelerators and other experiments which your physicists carry out are presently very unstable at your level of energy use. As you learn to use atomic energy creatively, they will become more stable and will eventually become a normal part of Earth's material substance. The subatomic particles symbolize your stretch to integrate more of the potential of the universe, your own potential, really, into your physical-plane, conscious reality.

In one sense then, the atomic particles of which your physical existence is formed are the basic substance with which you work at the physical level to expand your consciousness as a being of unlimited creative power. Your atomic physicists perform the service for the rest of you of organizing your present level of understanding of power into a system of knowledge of physical existence at the most basic level of consciousness. They are defining the abilities atoms have at this time to evolve and your ability to use them. They provide the conceptual framework of understanding that allows you to evolve your use of physical matter within your own evolutionary process. Earth provides the integral structure which holds physical existence within your sphere of experiencing as you explore it.

We said that your experience, your environment is a result of your thinking. Earth holds a focus for your thoughts which continue to grow and expand with you, providing the next level of experience as you grow in your understanding of how to create using physical matter. The One Supreme Creator, which we are calling Source, through Its supporting structure of highly developed cocreator-creators, has "thought" Earth into existence for the specific purpose of providing an arena for evolving consciousness. They have done part of the work of organizing physical existence into a coherent system for you to work with until you are able to create at a more cosmic level. Instead of having to deal with the whole universe at once in your learning, you first work with a piece of it.

There was a time in your evolution when you worked at a more basic level and were involved in the building and operation of your own physical body only. Few on Earth are now still at that level. You have perfect the use of your physical bodies to the point where they run themselves quite nicely, with the help of your subconscious. The rudimentary parts of your brain deal with your body's basic functions, with coordinating the activity in your cells themselves. You don't have to give any conscious attention to breathing, digesting your food, etc. Any problems in the operation of your body are the result of stresses and misprogramming originating at emotional and mental levels. These problems may arise in this lifetime, but usually are the result of misunderstandings that have arisen in past lifetimes or experiences in sequential time upon which this life's experiences depend.

Your body now can function well enough by itself to allow you to devote most of your consciousness to matters outside yourselves. This is allowing you to expand the framework of your consciousness beyond your own self. You are beginning to see that what you are goes beyond your own body and includes, ultimately, the whole Earth, maybe even the whole universe. You are seeing that what you do affects not only yourself, but also your world. You are learning that your thoughts affect not only your environment, but your family, your society, everyone. Earth provides the means of "keeping it all together" until you can develop a consciousness that is broad enough to do it yourself.

Does Earth, as a physical entity, know it is doing this? Not really, we are taught. It is a collection of physical particles held together by its own higher consciousness for the purpose of expanding its awareness of itself in a divine sense. It is learning to understand itself piece by piece. It is so vast a collection of individual conscious entities (the elemental particles) that it must integrate them piece by piece, step by step. Many other conscious entities who have learned to use physical matter as a cohesive unit become the steps by which Earth integrates herself. You are not yet able to integrate the functioning and existence of a whole planet into your conscious awareness, but you do know enough to take a portion of Earth's physical matter and organize it into a form that can support consciousness at the physical level. You have learned to enlist the support of the individual atoms that make up your cells into more complex molecules which then form the structure of your body. At one point in your evolution you had to make a conscious connection with the consciousness of each atom that became a part of your physical structure. You had to literally ask each atom to work with you. You had to make friends with each one and "persuade" it to become a part of your evolution. Fortunately, most atoms are quite ready to work with you because they recognize that they will also grow with you in consciousness.

You help Earth now by taking responsibility for some of her substance and teaching it to become part of a larger, world consciousness. That is what your evolution is all about. Your consciousness is expanding, your understanding of yourself as a divine being is expanding, your ability to create is expanding. You share this expansion with Earth by sharing the expansion process with her. Incidentally, each atom has a higher self, just as you do, which guides its evolution from a more cosmic perspective. One atom cannot learn to see itself as the universe without the step-by-step expansion process any more than you can. Your soul becomes its teacher in expanding its awareness, just as your spiritual teachers lead you into an awareness of how to be a creative part of a group. The Earth limits your perspective, but that limitation allows you to explore your potential in easy stages.

When you end one period of existence at the physical level, a part of the souls of the atoms which were part of your body become integrated into what has been called a "seed atom." Some of the consciousness of all the atoms is integrated into one atomic consciousness which remembers what it was like to be part of your physical body. Each lifetime adds to this seed the learning of each atom and the knowledge of how to use any higher energies you learned to use in that life. Your seed atom becomes part of the structure of physical existence which your soul has learned to use consciously. The atoms are evolving by sharing in your growth experiences. They lose individual consciousness, yes, but those that work with you become unique because of your uniqueness.

The atoms that become part of Earth are imprinted with her experience and learning also. The atoms that were a part of your body go back into the Earth and give up their learning to your soul but they do not lose what they give up. It also becomes part of Earth's experience. Your individual contribution from one lifetime may seem minuscule, but you have been here many times, had many bodies — thousands of them. Added up they become a considerable influence on Earth's "thinking." As you learn to combine your efforts with other's, you each reinforce what the others do. You build up a reservoir of knowledge within physical matter simply by working with it for a long time. You become used to it and know it very well in familiar circumstances. To the extent you have been able to work with others and share the learning, experiencing process with them, you also share their learning.

You know how to combine and manipulate matter to create what you need. You started with simple things like food and worked up to buildings and machines. As your ability to mentally conceive new ideas grew, you worked them into the physical level and created there. Not all of what you created benefited everyone, and not all was in harmony with the Divine Plan, but that is part of the learning process. The point now is, are you willing to look at everything you have learned and all that you have created, take responsibility for it, and choose what you want to keep? If you can learn to look deep into yourselves at everything you have done and learned, you have the opportunity to take what is useful and let go of the rest. Sometimes you have so much buried guilt about everything that didn't work that you refuse to look at what you have done that did work. This blocks out your memory of failure but also your knowledge of your growing power. The fear that power must always be destructive can keep you from seeing that you have learned much about using it creatively and usefully.

You are also blocking your power when you refuse to recognize at all levels that you are part of Earth. When you block that connection, you block the knowledge gained by being part of Earth. For each one of you, at least a few of those fractured parts of yourself that are immersed in anger, grief, hate, loneliness, and hopelessness are refusing to connect into your power at the physical level. They don't want to be hurt again. They are afraid of doing it wrong again. They are sure there is no point in trying again because Earth cannot accept love and use it positively. These parts of yourself are thinking anger, grief, hate, loneliness, and hopelessness. They are creating situations in your life that reflect these conditions and any others that are part of your experience that you have buried and don't want to look at, but which are still part of you.

Your Christian Bible says that Jesus Christ gave his life so your sins would be forgiven. Let's look at that this way, because it is important. When you accept that you are Light and love, as he did, and when you accept responsibility for all aspects of yourself including recognition that you are Light and love, you have the opportunity to create whatever you want. If you choose to create punishment for your mistakes you will continue to experience a life that is not what you ultimately would like it to be. When you decide to create a life of Light and love, you open to the universal flow of Light and love which the Creator is constantly sending you. You realize that no one punishes you but yourself, and you see that you can forgive yourself as the Creator already has and begin to allow yourself to use Source Light to create in pure love, without judgment or limitation. Eliminating the guilt allows you to move into a creative rather than a destructive pattern for your life.

That was the message of your Christ as we see it, to allow yourselves to be so filled with Light that every part of self can use what you have learned about physical existence to explore your growing creativity. He was the first to see, from the physical perspective, that the physical matter of Earth is capable of being an integral part of that universal flow of Light from Source. His realization was built on the accumulated knowledge of many spiritual masters before him, but his contribution was special and shared with physical Earth herself the knowledge that her Light is the same Light that flows from Source Itself. And now, as each of you begins to think Light and love and is willing to release from self all thoughts, conscious or subconscious, of darkness in yourself, you also share that with Earth.

But you must love Earth and your physicality and accept them as part of yourself. If you deny that you are fully a part of that, you block your connection to the power of what you have learned here. You cannot become a master at the physical level if you accept only what has seemed to work and what you can accept of your experience here. That creates a division within self which doesn't allow you to use all of the creativity Source has given you. Now that is okay if that is what you want. But you are still here struggling, so we must assume that some part of yourself does not want to leave any loose ends, any unintegrated parts behind. It will not take that much extra effort to gather your full creative potential as reflected in your Earth experience so that your soul has that power available to it. You began your Earth experience so you could learn as much as possible about your creative potential, and your soul is reminding you of that decision and giving you the opportunity to complete what you came here for.

You are not being forced to stay here by some authority outside yourself. At the end of each life you have an opportunity to return to unlimitedness or to return and gather more of the power you have lost in physical existence through apparent failure and dissociation from its difficult areas. You have consistently chosen to regain your power so that you can finally, one day, return to Source with more than you left with. You want to give to Source the ultimate gift, your expanded creativity, because you are Source and Source is unlimited. To limit your ability to expand would be to deny your Source identity.

So we are here with many others to help you gather up the pieces of your creative power and recreate your wholeness through building a better planet, a new Earth. Earth, as we said, is a focusing point for the thoughts of all those divine, cosmic beings who are supporting what you are doing here. Earth hasn't always been able to flow all this divine help in the ideal way, but as each one of you has learned to work with your spiritual teachers, you have become part of the Earth that does know how to do that. Enough of this alignment with the Divine Plan has been encoded into Earth's physical atoms that she is now able collectively to serve as that focus for divine intention which will guide and support you as you become more and more a part of the flow of divine Light and love at a conscious level.

We see the ascension of Christ as the critical point at which Earth began to become aligned with the Divine Plan at this coming, new energy level. There was enough connection to it that she herself could consciously support your service here. He left physical existence with much to be done, and there is still much to be completed, but there is a definite movement now toward integration of Light into physical existence that hasn't been available as a foundation for your love in all the eons of Earth's existence. You are not here just to define yourself as a divine being of Light. You are here to perfect your interaction with physical matter itself as a creative part of your divine Light. You are consciously making the physical atoms of Earth a part of your divine structure. Earth's physical matter is what provides the sub-stance of your expanded creativity. It is what is stretching you into an expansion of your creative power.

You are expanding your conscious awareness of the potential of physical existence itself by becoming part of it. Don't you agree that that is the best way to learn what it is and what it can do? Have you ever learned much by watching someone else? Can you learn what baseball really is by watching others play? Isn't it much more fun to play, yourself, even if you are not a pro? Don't you then have a greater understanding of what baseball really is? Don't you also have a greater appreciation of what the pros are doing if you have played yourself. Learning from life works the same way. You can't really enjoy it by watching it go by from your window. Yes, it is probably safer, and you will not make as many mistakes if you stay at home, but books and TV give a limited perspective. Daring to move out provides the perspective you are looking for, the opportunity to make Earth experience a real part of yourself.

Now Earth is able to provide more of the "Light experiences" you have been looking for. She is able to do that because you have taught her what you want and how to provide it. We are hoping that you will be able to maintain that opportunity you have created here to complete your mastery of physicality. We want to help you iron out the remaining details in creating your new Earth. Some of your problems seem insurmountable now, but if you can all mobilize your inner resources and collect your inner power, they can be solved very rapidly. Every part of yourself that learns to create the ideal is a part of yourself that is not recreating lack and disharmony on Earth. As you progress in the integration of your own power, you become an integrative focus for the ideal, literally a vortex of power for creating the ideal that can magnetically help others align into that focus. When you create a change in one part of the hologram that is Earth, the whole must change also.

We of Ataien reached a point in our own evolution where we realized, as one, that being physical meant we were one with our planet. This realization was made at all levels of our consciousness and allowed us to connect into our power in a way we had not conceived of before. It magnified our creative power thousands of times, ultimately, and provided the force needed to break out of the limits of physical existence while remaining within it. We not only regained our wholeness, becoming able to function as complete spiritual souls on our planet, but we also magnified our power through the unity in consciousness on our whole planet. This is what made it possible for us to explore other dimensions and to work with them without losing our power to them. Our concept of the structure of our Light is so sure and unified that nothing can disrupt its flow unless we choose to allow it.

You are working a little differently on your Earth. You are exploring your power from an individual perspective. This has made it difficult for you to connect into the whole in a way that makes your learning more comfortable but has allowed more diversity within the learning of the whole. As you now become able to use the support of the whole without losing your own identity you have a very broad spectrum of experience to draw into your expansion into being part of Earth as a creator with her. This is the completion at the physical level. We feel that our individual ability to use the knowledge and experience of the whole would help you bridge the gap between yourselves and the whole at the physical level. You already know how to return to the whole "vertically," by giving up your physical bodies and returning to the Light. Your challenge now is to recognize yourself as part of the whole at the physical level and to integrate physical existence into your knowledge that you are part of everything and everything is within you. Part of you knows that, but those parts that are a little disconnected cannot yet know that wholeness.

We are hoping that our sharing with you will allow us, not only to maintain human life within physical existence on your planet, but to help you realize the full potential of your power, individually and as a planet. Your planet is a key now to an expansion of your galaxy and ultimately of Source Itself. We want to be a part of that and we want to share our understanding of what that means. We want most to share our love with you. When any connection between two conscious beings is made in pure love and acceptance of each other, that is the most exhilarating experience of all and the most expanding. And we hope that by sharing ourselves and our goals with you in this way, we will eliminate the fear that prevents that complete sharing of love.

Meditation/Exercise

Create, mentally, some kind of symbol that represents Earth. It might be a circle or sphere, a star, or maybe a more complex geometric structure. Imagine that symbol is surrounded by light from many points streaming toward it. Earth and all the points of light are surrounded by a finer Light that radiates love and caring. As this Light is poured into Earth it grows slowly brighter. Now imagine other points of Light on, or in, Earth herself. These points are you and other Lightworkers living on Earth. Your Light is also doing its part to help Earth become brighter.

As Earth's Light grows, imagine all the radiant points making connections with each other. Each time a connection is made their radiance grows and more Light flows into Earth. Points of Light on Earth connect with each other and with those points of Light around Earth. The radiance grows, and as it does, imagine the growing feelings of love in its many aspects increasing around you as you create this picture. Feel more joy, more peace, more acceptance, caring, abundance, trust, enthusiasm, cooperation — whatever you would like to see added to Earth now.

The Light is growing brighter and brighter now. It seems to be almost exploding around you, expanding until it reaches out and begins to envelop those points of Light that were once outside it. They are becoming part of Earth now. And the radiance grows and grows. The feeling of love gets stronger and stronger and you feel more and more a part of every aspect of this picture as the love connects you into everything.

Focus that feeling of love into your heart and allow it to radiate from there. Know that you are supported in your Light, accepted as a source of Light, and that your Light is contributing to the expanding Light of Earth and the integration of what has not previously been part of your concept of Light here. Send that Light into every part of your body. Trust that every part of yourself is worthy of this Light. Know that this Light is what you really are. Know that this Light can be a way to appreciate your physical reality in a way you never have before. Let your heart and the love flowing from it connect you to everything and everyone around you with love. Try to maintain that feeling of love flowing from your heart when you are finished with this exercise. Practice making these Light-love connections whenever you can during your day.

Ranoash of Ataien

9

This is a new time for your Earth. There are more new opportunities than have ever been available before. As you begin to be able to see what is available and to understand the changes that are occurring, you will begin to see more clearly just how you fit into this pattern of change and how these changes benefit you. Even now, you are more able to assimilate new ideas than ever before. This is partly because of the expansion of your mental capabilities, but also because there is an energy structure within the Earth itself which is supporting particular patterns of ideas.

Earth has reached a critical point of expansion where growth is no longer random but has found its place in the flow of the whole in a new way. Very long ago she learned to balance physically with the rest of the galaxy and universe. I mean that the laws that govern movement and position were mastered within the original structural plan of creation. These laws were the blueprint that laid down the basic building blocks at the physical level. In your solar system this established the position of your Sun within this galactic sector and the communicative links that connect it to the rest of the sector. It also allowed the formation of the planets and delineated their specific purposes in the Solar System. Once the structural framework of the physical level was established you gradually expanded it through emotional, then mental explorations.

Each planet had its own part to play in the developing intelligence of the system. The knowledge which originates at the Source, or universal level, is stepped down into incremental units which can be placed into the specific areas being explored at every level — subuniversal, galactic, solar, planetary and, finally, individual. Each level uses less of the broad picture and more of specific areas of creative potential which Source-as-All wishes to explore. This knowledge flows as Light and is the manifestation of Source's love. The energy flows most slowly at the level of planets in physical form, yet development is faster there. The energy flow of the Sun is higher, but its level of growth or thought encompasses a broader perspective. Having more to deal with in its understanding, its cycles are more cosmic and thus much longer. The galactic and universal flows move faster but the magnitude of the cycles is even further from our comprehension. Realizations, or milestones, in understanding are made once every thousand or million years.

At the level of consciousness that is human on your Earth, the detailed viewpoint provides the opportunity to make many realizations about yourself and who you are and to take many steps in your understanding in one lifetime or series of lifetimes. At first these milestones came only every thousand years. As your knowledge about physical existence grew, there was more to draw from as you began to integrate it and put together the puzzle of who you are from a physical viewpoint. Every experience provides a new piece of the puzzle. Some of the pieces fit and some don't. It is up to you to build your picture of who you are from your own reservoir of experience. You have had the opportunity to try many things and to explore many of the variables and combinations of variables of your creativity.

This exploration of your creative potential at the physical level takes place against the background of your soul's purpose. That provides the framework within which you explore. When you remain close to that framework you feel supported and things seem to move easily. When you venture outside that framework you feel lost and confused and movement can be very difficult. Sometimes the ease of the movement within the framework seems to propel you outside it. Things may be going very well, but suddenly you find yourself in a space where things are not going well. Your soul may very well have moved you into an area that it does not understand but wants to learn about. It cannot guide you in the details of how to function in unknown territory, but it does maintain a connection that allows you to find your way out of your difficulty. Hopefully you will have learned something useful which your soul can use and which adds to your understanding of life and yourself.

Sometimes you forget your soul connection and thus lose the guidance which could take you out of the difficult area. Other times you feel that your soul has led you into "darkness" and left you to struggle alone. At the time you do not see the value of the difficult experience and you blame soul for getting you into uncomfortable circumstances. You may get very angry with your soul and even feel that it doesn't know very much or is refusing to see that you need help.

When you were a very young aspect of your soul, it nurtured you very carefully, watching every move like a mother caring for a toddler. Now you are quite mature. You have experienced much of life at the physical level. Like any adult you must learn to take responsibility for your life if you are to become a productive, creative member of the cocreator-creative whole. Your soul has accepted your ability to function purposefully at the physical level, "cut the apron strings," and is now allowing you to make your own decisions, to determine your own path. Does this mean it wants nothing more to do with you? Never! It is looking forward to the time when it can relate to you as a partner, one who can make his or her own creative contribution to Its purpose. It needs a partner who is adept at functioning at the physical level because it cannot.

If your soul is to accomplish its purpose of transforming physical matter into Light that flows in perfect harmony with the Divine Plan, it needs a physical vehicle which can provide a connection at the physical level and to its level of thought processes. You are not that physical structure, but you are the consciousness that knows how to use it. You are the connection between that structure and your soul. As a conscious unit, you have been very focused into working at the physical level. You have been busy putting together the pieces of your experience which explain what physical existence is and how it works.

You are also trying to understand what that means. For that you must maintain your physical perspective while turning to your soul, learning to integrate its perspective with your physical one. You must share with your soul and allow it to share with you. This sharing does not guarantee instant understanding of the universe and your place in it. It gives you glimpses of possible explanations of what life is and what it means. It gives you the germ of an idea which must be translated into a concept that has meaning at the physical level and which can be applied there. The sharing is not meant to take you out of physical existence, but to explain it in a way that expands your ability to use your creativity within it.

The great beings who ensoul our planet, sun, and galaxy have already gone through this process of learning how to work with physical existence. They have learned to maintain their connection to Source as a part of their active consciousness while they turn their focus toward the more specific functioning of creation's many aspects. In a sense, the strength that allows them to do what they are doing is their ability to see in front and in back at the same time, to see their individual tasks without feeling separated from the functioning of the whole, to always know how what they do affects the rest of creation while being very involved in their own specific tasks. They have not had the same experience you are having, and they may not even have gone as deeply into physical experience as you, but they can move the focus of their awareness from the very detailed physical one to the very expanded cosmic one without feeling any sense of discontinuity between them.

This ability to move in consciousness from one dimension to another is the next step for most of you, as developing cocreator-creators. You have probably made random connections into expanded awareness which you can recall and use at the physical level but are not yet able to maintain that connection at will. When you can, you will no longer be limited by your physical body but will be able to use it as a tool for expanding your knowledge of your potential. Then you will know, without doubt, that you are more than your physical body and you will be able to prove it to yourself at will. Miracles are just the ability to shape physical matter from a higher perspective. First you "make the acquaintance" of physical matter at its level and literally make it your own by integrating it into your physical body. Then you can move to a new, broader perspective of understanding where you integrate it into the pattern of Earth's ideal.

When you have reached that point, you are consciously working with the Divine Plan as a conscious cocreator-creator. You have the opportunity to make your own choices about how physical matter flows in that Plan. You also have the responsibility to see that your choices do not interfere with the ability of others to make their own choices. You also become aware of choices already made to cooperate with a specific direction that the Plan is taking. You have free will, but you do not always insist on using it. You learn to wait for the opportunity to work out some ideas at the appropriate "time."

This appropriate time may be a dimensional experience which is concurrent with this one. There have been many such extensions of Earth experience. My dimension is an extension of yours and yours is an extension of mine. Argument about which came first is really meaningless because time is one of the major illusions of creation. Ours might be regarded as first, in that we have a better connection into the higher-dimensional viewpoint which gives a broader understanding of evolution. Yours might be considered first in that your experience provides a purpose for our continuing existence. As our explorations led us to discover your world, we have gained knowledge about the reason for ours, the existence of ours.

Time is the key element now in your expanding understanding of your place in the whole. The illusion of time allows you to view actions and their consequences. You are moving out of an extremely focused point of view from which you see only one very small part of creation, the one you are viewing at this particular moment in space and time as you have created it. You have not been placed here by some higher element of consciousness that is randomly manipulating you through the maze of some meaningless "chess game." Remember, we said you have created your own reality. You think out every element of your existence. The fact that you cannot remember doing that, when or how it began, or how it works is incidental. What is important is that you are beginning the process of remembering. You are remembering the original causes that placed you exactly where you are. As you recreate your actions and their results, you can begin to act in a way that brings the result you are looking for.

First you must begin to remember who you are, that you are divine consciousness with free will. You must understand what that means and that there are no limits placed on your creativity. Then you must begin the process of unraveling the creative process that brought you here. It is no longer good enough to randomly make decisions at the physical level which are unrelated to your soul's purpose or to the Divine Plan. Decisions must now include a higher perspective if your life is to begin to make sense and if you are to begin to see that you really are in control of it. But you say, "I don't know who I am. I don't know why I am here. Prove to me I have a soul that can guide me with an understanding of how I am supposed to fit into this supposed cosmic Plan. I am very confused and this is making no more sense than my life ever has. I have suffered intolerable pain and loneliness. Life keeps dumping more nasty stuff on me even though I try to imagine that I am divine . I try to see myself as Light and all I get is some very short moments, perhaps, of Light, if I am lucky. Then I again find myself on an Earth that is full of hunger, greed, pain, disease and seemingly unlimited suffering. If I created this I certainly am a lousy example of a creator. It is not what I want."

Well, first let me say things are not as bad as they look. I know your Earth seems to be very sick, even dying. I know your whole system of civilization, economic, social, and moral, is about to collapse. I know you sometimes have a very difficult time seeing how you can possibly get through this alive, much less how you can create something better out of it. But you can. Your Earth has been destroyed many times; all life has vanished from her surface. Yet she remains, a sparkling gem in a far corner of one small galaxy, which beckons to the universe, "Come and share my Light. Help me show you what I can really do." Her potential remains, clear and challenging, visible to all who want to explore love and use it to create. It has never disappeared for an instant. Her courage drives her to try again to express what she knows is within. Every new beginning has been more challenging than the last because of the accumulated wisdom of all previous experiences.

It is the same for you. You have tried many ways of sharing your creativity with the Divine Plan. You have explored every aspect of your potential in countless ways. Some things worked and some didn't seem to. It is all recorded someplace in your consciousness, when you can but reach it. The narrow focus you are now using limits your ability to do that. But every memory of every event is just one example of what your creativity might be. Until you choose to place it in the fabric of this life, it does not exist for you here. When you begin to put together the elements of your creativity from an expanded perspective you can use that new perspective of physical existence to create from a more knowledgeable one.

In the process of weaving your present understanding of who you are as a creator, you choose each element of your past experiencing and knowledge and examine it. Some things are not completely understood and must be looked at many times. Some must be reworked before they are useful to you now. Each is a part of your potential creativity and contains an investment of your energy. Each has resulted in some sort of structure's being left in physical existence. That is where your purpose is directed and that is where your efforts are recorded.

The present discovery of the necessity of recycling your resources is symbolic of what you must do to make sense out of your Earth experience. Just as you appear to have limited resources and ability to deal with waste in your environment, the whole of your Earth experience must be converted into something useful in expressing your creativity. Everything that you have ever done and learned has some place in the pattern of your creativity. If your actions were not helpful to your divine purpose, you must look to see what you need to change to make them so. You must correct the direction of each action so you create what you intend. That is what your life here is about and always has been about. You are constantly reworking the pattern of your actions so they fit more closely within the flow of the Divine Plan.

Over and over, you rework each aspect of your creative potential, slowly mastering the use of your potential.

You are perfectionists. You have come together many times to help each other recreate your methods of working within the Divine Plan. You work alone and together, looking at how to create what you want and how to use it. One of your biggest problems is to see when you can release what doesn't work without ignoring your responsibility for changing it. Even when you have rebuilt something so that it more clearly expresses what you wanted, you often retain the memory of the previous attempt. Part of your energy goes into maintaining that old structure. "Well, I need it to remind me of what not to do." Or maybe, "I might not have gotten all I need from that. I might have missed something." " I want to get it exactly right, so I must keep all my experiences in case I think of a better way later."

Stop wasting your energy and creative power on regrets and what might have been. That holds part of your creative energy back into maintaining what did not work. Releasing that power into your present endeavors is the first step in channeling all your power into what you are doing now. Then allow yourself to view what you are doing in the light of your original intention, as much as you can understand it. When you do this you may discover your intention has changed somewhat. The original problem may have changed. That doesn't mean what you have done already is wasted. It means you are seeing it differently. Your experience in working with it has allowed you to see it in a new way. You can now see a new way of working with it. You may see a whole new goal and understand more of your original purpose. You must stop periodically to evaluate your progress and reassess your plan. This is the procedure for reaching any goal.

Achieving your soul's purpose works the same way, but you often don't see that. If you reach a block or a stopping place you feel you have failed. Or perhaps you think your spiritual guidance has failed. Death provides opportunities for re-evaluating your progress, but when you die you often divide yourself. You give the best of your accomplishments to your soul and feel that since you have to work out the problems left, they are what you are. You forget that what you give to your soul becomes a bridge between you and soul. It becomes the strength which supports you as you begin again to work out each area of learning in physical existence. It is always available to you as well as to your soul although you each view it from a different perspective.

This sharing occurs as a major evaluation point at death, but it can also occur often during your life. In fact, as your perspective expands, it may no longer be necessary to die in order to assess your progress. That is what is happening now. You have the opportunity to redirect your movement and learning during this life. It takes conscious awareness and thought about what needs to be changed. You don't have to leave physical existence to contact the guidance of your spiritual teachers and change your direction. They are here for you now whenever you need them. Just ask for guidance and it is there, perhaps not in the way you expected, but it will always come if you ask. The same applies to any request for help. It won't come if you don't ask and it is never denied. What happens if you ask for the wrong thing? What if your evaluation of what is needed does not help evolve the Divine Plan? It probably won't work very well. That doesn't mean the advice or your application of it was bad. It means you need to re-evaluate your method of reaching your goal. It means you have learned something new which will now allow you to create a new plan for reaching your goal. Ask again; more help will come. It will come in a way that helps you see a better way of moving toward it.

Source intended that physical existence should support your growing creativity. That means it is designed to support the process of learning how to use it. You will not be punished for mistakes, but if you choose to mire yourself in them and regret your actions you will be punishing yourself by remaining in a situation you have created which does not support your progress. Decide you can now try again to create something better and the whole creative system will support you. Have you ever noticed how exciting new projects are? There is always the hope that each will be better. That hope and the energy of your decision to act carry you forward and bring you what you need. What you need to realize is that the creative support system allows you to change your mind. If it did not, there could be no learning through experience. Re-evaluating and recreating the path to your goal is part of the process.

The point is, Earth is supporting the creative process and your understanding of it more than ever before. The creative flow is moving faster and faster. It is like the assembly line in an automated factory. The belt moves faster as your ability to assimilate your experience and grow in your understanding increase. The energy available for creative purposes is coming faster and faster and creating change, whether you choose to work with it or not. It will destroy what has been because that has completed its purpose. What was created for learning must be replaced by the next lesson. If you work with it you can use the energy to recreate your place on Earth to suit your divine purpose. If you sit and watch it go by it will take your chance to create something better with it.

Well, that is what most of you are trying to do, but I think it would be helpful to define the process a bit. This is a time to be very clear in your intent, to allow your understanding of the creative process to grow in harmony with the changing energies, and to make frequent assessments of your progress. That is one reason why there is so much spiritual help available now: not to make the changes for you, but to help you reach beyond your physical-plane viewpoint into the deeper aspects of your creative potential. Your other-dimensional friends are here to help you stretch into greater use of your strengths, to help you create opportunities to use them and to understand your part in the whole Plan. As you reach out to connect with what seems to be outside yourself, you connect with more of what is inside yourself. You cannot really use anything that is not already yours.

The reaching out is a part of the process of expanding yourself. Every spiritual teacher you work with represents a different part of your creative potential. That is why their messages come differently through each person. And, that is why you are encouraged to work with many teachers rather than just one. Many times you find yourself cut off from a very comfortable relationship with a favorite spiritual teacher and encouraged to work with another. You may feel that your old teacher has left you unsupported, but your soul will be there guiding you into a new friendship that will help you see your potential in a new way. It is not that the old teacher was limited, but that your habitual way of working with him or her limited your ability to move into a new area of self-exploration.

Earth is providing an anchoring point for the attention of many new energies and ideas. This is making available to you the ideas of many different groups and some very cosmic individuals. There is a multitude of new ideas for recreating your environment on Earth. Each new consciousness brings not only new ideas but new energy, new movement, because thought creates movement and movement is energy. Fortunately, the ideas of these new friends of Earth are aligned, each in its own way, with the Divine Plan. They intensify its flow, making it easier to find and connect with. They are, in fact, making it almost impossible to miss. If you have any intention at all of working with it, you will be caught up in its flow and become a part of It.

What is new, as of July of 1992, is that Earth itself has become connected into that flow in a new way. In August of 1987, the Divine Plan made a connection into Earth at the physical level. This began a process of change which is moving faster and deeper. In July 1992, Earth "figured out" how to flow with that connection. All of you who were looking for ways to help move with the new energies helped in that alignment process. Now that it is accomplished, it is easier to see your place in the flow. You are beginning to find things easier to understand and changes easier to make. It is only a beginning but a focus is available that wasn't there before because Earth can now help you hold the connection to the Plan more clearly.

In 1995 there will be another important alignment when the ideas available will become clearer in terms of your physical perspective. What now seem to be elusive ideals will become clear possibilities. Purpose will be clearer and the means of attaining it will be obvious. As you continue to make the adjustments necessary to reaching that goal and as you work to make yourself a clearer channel for the Light of the Divine Plan, you will be helping to create that opening. The cosmic intelligence which is now focusing the Plan more intensely for

Earth will become a more a part of physical-plane awareness. The pieces of the puzzle will suddenly fit. Change will become, even more, a way of life, but the changes will have more meaning for you.

As your understanding of the Plan becomes clearer, you will gain confidence in the power of your thoughts. As more of you reach a clearer awareness of the Plan, the unity of your thoughts will create a more powerful flow of its Light at the physical level. The challenge then will become to allow that Light to flow through you. As you observe the effects of the Plan's flow on Earth you can work together to direct it in the most efficient way possible. You will learn to act as soul's body in carrying it out. Your job will not be to drop out and let soul do it, but to work with soul, providing the physical actions necessary. Your thoughts will become, eventually, so aligned with soul's purpose in the Plan that you will act at its direction without any breaks in its flow. Your mind will have expanded to include more of soul's knowledge and understanding. You will still function differently at the physical level than you would if you did not have a physical body. Your understanding will not be complete, because that will not yet be possible on the physical level on Earth. But you will be moving toward that more complete understanding and may even decide to stick around in physical existence to see how far Earth can go in allowing that more complete awareness of your potential to be present here with you.

10

We have talked a lot about potential — yours and Earth's. What is your potential anyway? You know that somehow you are supposed to be divine, even though you don't really feel like that. How would it feel to really know you are divine and still physical? What would be different? For example, how would a God create its reality if it were in physical existence? Any being who attains god-powers seems to leave the physical to work from some other level. What are the elements of creative power? This may seem like going over old material once again, but the aspects of love are the elements of creative power.

We said that Source is unlimited love; so It creates with love because of Its love for Itself. We said that you on Earth have been looking at love from every possible angle in order to learn about it. We said you have explored it in extraordinary ways, including trying to see love from a point outside love. Now this is not really possible unless you become something other than what you are, something other than part of Source. But physical existence seems to provide that outside viewpoint in that you don't know, when you first enter it, how to use love there. The only way to do that is to create the patterns within it through which love can flow physically. Sexual love has been one of the patterns developed quite intensively. It allowed you to combine the physical body and your emotions into an activity involving love. Your minds are still finding out how to enter into that pattern. You will eventually learn that your whole being, at all levels, can be an expression of love.

We also said that the Plan for physical existence is already in place here and is being focused by the thoughts of beings at many levels who hold the concept of creation in their minds. So the patterns you require to use love here must already be in place. For some reason, you just can't see them. The Plan for creation is radiating as the love of Source pervading the universe. Since you are part of Source, isn't it also radiating as love from you? We usually think of love as originating in the heart. Could the love radiating from your heart really be the love of Source creating the universe? Then the universe for each of you originates in your hearts. Is each universe as different as you are from each other? The answer is yes.

And what's more, there are billions, even trillions, of these universal realities interacting within the same space and time. Source, as the whole which existed before any separation, is focusing Its reality. There are twelve very experienced cocreator-creators who understand that original concept perfectly, as far as we can see, although sometimes there are slight variations, because they are each still individuals, after all. The differences do not arise out of disagreement, ego concerns, or even ignorance. They are simply the result of random variations which occur within Source since its elements are infinite in number. Remember, it separated into parts to explore the potential of these differing elements within itself. Not only are there differences within each individual consciousness, but there are unlimited ways to express each difference.

Let's say a child decides to skip school for a day. It has many choices of what to do. It can go to the park, fool around at the mall, go to a show, stay home and watch TV, or hitch-hike to L.A. Each choice has the potential of changing the child's life in some way. Some choices are much riskier than others. The randomness is expressed in the child's decision to depart from the original plan. The Divine Plan works something like that, in that there are always choices to be made, because no one knows exactly how a creative experience will turn out. We always include some unknown elements in creation or there would be no reason to explore it in the first place. And the Plan gives each one the structure needed to support the choice.

Each cocreator-creator, developing ones as well as those approaching Source-level comprehension of creation, has free will. That is the
defining part of the unlimitedness we carry with us when we "separate" from Source. The only way to move is to make choices. Whether
we know we have free will or not, we are always required to make
choices. We can "choose" our way into all sorts of adventures and
difficulties and we can then choose to remain in them or go on to
something else. More importantly, we can choose to act out of ignorance of our Source qualities. If we choose to act as part of Source, we
must act out of love. So we have come around again to the problem
we started with. If we forget who we are when we become physical,
how can we act with love? How do we find the Divine Plan and align
with it if we can't see it, feel it, hear it, if there is no evidence it exists,
as some on Earth have claimed?

We have trillions or more units of individual consciousnesses, each
with an individual point of view from which its reality is evolving. Each
one is constantly making its own choices, determining its own path.
Overlaid on all this is the Divine Plan, there to guide any who are aware
of it and choose to follow it. As all these realities interact, they have the
potential to affect those around them. You might imagine the universe
to be something like an enormous orchestra tuning up. At first each
player is involved in checking out his or her own instrument and there
is what sounds like total chaos or dissonance. Then the concertmaster
rises, signals for silence, the oboe sounds its note and the entire orchestra tunes each instrument to correspond to it. There is another brief
interlude of chaotic sound before the conductor enters, as each player
checks to see that his instrument is properly tuned with the whole
orchestra. The maestro raises his baton; there is silence; then the
harmonies begin to come forth.

When you go to a concert, you hear the final result of weeks or
maybe months of rehearsing. Have you ever attended a concert given
by an elementary school band or orchestra? Any resemblance to real
harmony seems to be entirely coincidental. But the players are trying
very hard to play the music correctly and follow the conductor. They
have worked hard and practiced a lot to be able to do what they can at

this stage. The junior high or high school concerts show great improvement and there is a much more harmonious result. By the time players have developed their skills enough to join a major orchestra they have also learned much about working with a group under the direction of one authority, the conductor, as well as mastering their own instrument. Some conductors follow only their own preferences in interpreting the music. Others listen to the ideas of members of the orchestra and take them into account. Each member acts as an individual under the guidance of the conductor, but the effect is one of harmonious agreement as to the outcome.

Our Source is something like the conductor who listens to the members of the orchestra when he makes his interpretive decisions. Every part of this Source has an opportunity to contribute to the Plan if we choose to. At first we have enough trouble just getting a proper note from our instrument, our creativity. We don't have time or inclination to worry about interpretation. The finer nuances of musicality are beyond our capabilities anyway. As we develop our skills, our reality begins to take on a meaningful shape and character. We begin to look to the Plan for interpretive guidance just as an orchestra looks to its conductor to lead it to its highest potential for creating beautiful sounds.

That is about where Earth and you are now. You have gained reasonable control over your creative skills. You have bodies that work reasonably well without much attention on your part. You have family, social, and political systems that form the structure of your interaction with others. You are looking for some guidance that will give real meaning to your reality, something that will allow more harmony and beauty in the flow of your life. The Divine Plan is your "conductor" but you have to listen for Its guidance with your heart.

Your heart is the center of your being where your Source connection is hidden under the cover of your forgetfulness and ignorance of how to express your love which Source is always sharing with you. Just as love is always radiating from Source unlimitedly, so it flows from your heart, shaped by your choices. At the end of the last chapter, we said that you are learning to observe the Plan as it flows through you, so that you can take part in decisions about how it should continue its flow. It flows through you as love and love is what you observe. It doesn't look like love? You haven't yet gone deep enough into your heart, to what you really are, to see that love clearly. It is covered up by your confusion about how to create and layers of doubts about your creative ability arising out of creative experiences which did not turn out as you had hoped they would.

But at the center of your being you are still Source, divine Creator, unlimited love. The perfect ideal of the Divine Plan is there, coded into every aspect of your being. Just as the musician works for years to perfect his or her ability to play beautiful music, so you have worked for many lifetimes to develop and perfect your creative skills. Loving what you do is the key. You are learning to love yourself, to act out of love, to use love in many ways. Practicing and working with love is what will lead you to the answers you are looking for. Love is not only coming to you from Source through every aspect of your reality, it is coming from within you, unlimitedly. It is the power that creates your existence. As you work with this flow you become more adept in its use and it begins to do what you want it to do. When you learn to recognize that love is truly the substance of harmonious creative action, it begins to make sense and become easier.

You are really learning to work with love whether you realize it or not. And you have come further than you might think. That is why more of you are really focusing on love and its importance. You want love to be a part of your life. You have learned that if you find the right person, you might have the ideal relationship that is totally loving and supportive. Believe it or not, every one of you has, in some life, experienced such an ideal relationship. One reason you can't continue to repeat that experience is that you expected always to have someone else to provide a loving relationship, not recognizing that everything comes from within and you generate that ideal from inside yourself. Ultimately, you will be able to experience an ideal relationship with everyone. Every communication will result in ecstasy when you have found all the love in yourself.

You were not created feeling incomplete and unlovable. You created those feelings of imperfection as you tried to understand love and how to expand your use of it. Originally you knew that you were loved by Source and the universe was full of love. That knowledge is still part of you and you are rediscovering it. You have had many great teachers who have reminded you of what you are and who showed you how to live that ideal. If you keep the focus of that ideal, the structure you have built on incomplete knowledge and misperceptions about yourself will gradually be replaced by the ideal. As your vision of the ideal guides you, you must learn to clear out whatever does not allow it to be present. It is like building a house. First the land must be cleared and a foundation dug. Then you gather the materials and begin building. If that house becomes too small for what you have created, you can tear it down and build another. Actually, you sell it, take what you invested in it and get another, bigger one.

If you want a life of beauty and joy, full of love, you must discover what is in yourself that is blocking that. What do you dislike about yourself? What needs to be changed? Be realistic. Don't expect to build your house in a day. Don't waste time on a huge mansion if you only need a two-room house. Decide on what you want to do first. Is impatience with your progress creating so much frustration with yourself that you feel you are accomplishing nothing and your life is futile? Then begin by accepting yourself, even what you don't like.

Imagine that impatience is part of the structure on which your life is built. Begin to look at all the things you are impatient with and see how you can begin to accept and love them. Replace the impatience in your structure with acceptance and love for everything and everyone around you. If you honestly can feel you have done what you can for now, accept yourself also. If you look hard enough, you can always find something to love about everything and everyone. Focus on that. See if that reflects something in yourself that you can love. Remember, you are seeing yourself reflected in others. You can only really understand what is already within yourself. Gradually, your life will begin to seem acceptable. As you feel this acceptance of your life, your creative structure will cease to vibrate with the disharmony of impatience.

Ranoash of Ataien

You have all the time you need to solve each problem, because time is part of the reality that you create. Create it however you want. If your life is full of grief, look for things to be happy about. Make a point of looking for happiness wherever you can find it and learn to use it in your life. If you are always angry, look for ways to channel your desires constructively. Don't wait for someone else to do it. Only you can fulfill your own desires. The structure of your life is built of what you feel about everything you do. That structure is radiating from you in all directions. That structure is what is interacting with everything around you. If your structure is vibrating with the disharmonies of negative emotion, you are generating more disharmony. If you begin to fill your structure with the vibrations of love and its many aspects, your note will begin to blend into the whole more harmoniously and your environment will be reflected back to you as a comfortable, pleasant place to be.

Imagine that as every conscious being in the universe is generating the structure of its own environment, everything eventually interacts with everything else. If each structure is vibrating with love as its note, all notes will generate harmony. When some of the lines of various structures are vibrating with negative emotion, dissonances are created in the music the universe is generating. By now, you know which harmonies are pleasing to you and which you wish to avoid. You can continue to tune your note, your structure, so that it blends with the whole harmoniously. Then you can begin to explore the finer nuances of the song of creation, exploring its beauty, symmetry, and radiance. Your structure will be supported by the harmonies rather than weakened and shattered by dissonances.

"Listen" for the sound of your note as it mingles with other notes. Your note is sounding from your place in the Plan. Your spiritual teachers understand that Plan more clearly than you do at the physical level. Together, they are are the oboe, sounding the reference tone against which you can tune the structure of your experiencing. The orchestra of creation continues the warming up of each instrument, even while the rehearsal continues and the harmonies become clearer and surer. This is possible because we are not dealing with only one dimension but, possibly, an infinite number. You are creator and created. You are perfect in your Source origin while you are growing into knowledge of that perfection. You are love even while you look at what it is to be outside love. You remain in perfect harmony with All That Is even while you explore that harmony by disrupting it.

The center of your being is multidimensional. The outside is whatever dimension you choose to look at. When you have adjusted each dimension so that it is in harmony with the whole, you are consciously aware that it is part of your multidimensional center. Your conscious understanding of what comprises that center expands and you can use what is there with the confidence born from the familiarity achieved.

Your center is your potential. It is the unlimited elements of Source, arranged in a way that is unique to you and your experience. It is within you and you learn to use it bit by bit. At first it radiated from you as pure Light and love, but you chose not to claim it until you had explored it thoroughly. As you learned to use it in a way that created harmony with the rest of creation it became a part of you that you understood very well, well enough to feel confident in making your own decisions about its use. At first it was difficult and that pure Light radiated from you, in your sight, as something dark and inharmonious. Now, as it begins to blend in with the ideal, it is becoming light. You are seeing the Light that was there all along, but you didn't recognize it because you didn't understand it.

Your potential is infinite, but you must develop it piece by piece. The universe is "divided up" into many dimensions so you can do that. You have done much work in many dimensions. Now you are bringing those dimensions together as you pick up the pieces of your potential and integrate them into what you are doing on Earth. The dimensions that began to come together for Earth at the Harmonic Convergence are the dimensions of your experiencing. If you were not ready to integrate them there would not have been any Harmonic Convergence. You created it by your readiness to move beyond your third-dimensional understanding of what you are. You are tired of working on pieces of yourself and are ready to put the pieces together.

And so the pieces are here now for you.

Adjustments must be made in some pieces so they will fit into your Earth experience. Many of you recognize these parts of self that are well developed but haven't been used on Earth. They sometimes make you feel that you don't belong here, because they don't fit. That doesn't mean there is anything wrong with you or Earth. If you view your environment with love and act out of love as best you can, you can figure out how to make each piece fit in and help create the Earth that supports you and your ideal.

The Earth is quite flexible in its interpretation of the Divine Plan. It was intended to support you in discovering your full potential and can be adapted to many viewpoints, as long as they are in harmony with the Plan being used by the whole. Right now your main concern is to create an Earth which can support everyone's creativity and that is also the intention of the Plan. As you develop your potential, Earth develops hers also.

Love is magnetic. That is not just a meaningless expression, but a scientific fact. If Light is an electrical flow, then the love that created that Light becomes the magnetic field which is generated around it. The term "electromagnetic" implies just that. It combines the electrical flow and its magnetic field, Light and its magnetism, into the unity that they are. They are the stuff of which creation is built. The science of physics is describing metaphysical concepts, exploring them, and proving them.

Love moves as Light and attracts Light to it through its magnetism. That is how the Plan evolves Itself. It attracts everything that is Light to it, allowing it to align with It. The more you use love, the more love you attract to yourself. The more you use love, the more you create harmonious interactions with others and the more harmonic vibrations you generate. Acting without love isolates you from the rest of creation. It pushes you away from the Light, away from the support of the Divine Plan.

Earth has chosen to vibrate as pure love. This has made her a magnetic center for attracting many aspects of love from many dimensions and spaces of the universe. It provides an almost overwhelming choice of experiences, but also the magnetism necessary to pull them together. You must support that diversity with your acceptance and love of what is different as well as what is familiar. If Earth is to develop her full potential as a planet which vibrates to unlimited love, each of you must release your prejudices about what is acceptable and what is not acceptable to you. Your fear and hatred of what is different must be cleared out of your physical cells as well as out of your mind and emotions.

Your DNA was designed to be very flexible and to blend with many different types. Your decision to make one particular physical form your one ideal has limited the ability of your DNA to adapt to change. Your form has served as the best one for this time and place, but it is not the only useful one and when it has served its purpose it must be allowed to change. Taking this particular form to its highest expression of Light is not your only purpose and expresses only a small part of your potential. Your isolation in this third dimension has not allowed you to see the wisdom and knowledge gained within other forms. It has led to the misperception that trying to combine your DNA with that of other life forms creates monsters that are not capable of sustaining worthwhile life, or any life at all.

In reality, each life form has its strengths and weaknesses. You have lived in many forms in your many lives in this universe and others. This is merely the form you are working with now. It has taken you eons to bring it to this level of perfection. It has required much concentrated effort at the physical level. Now you must take it to a new level, if you are going to continue to work within this Plan. That is what your higher aspects are working for. This new level requires more adaptability to new energies and acceptance of them. It requires integrating these new energies into your physical body.

Does this mean your body will become strange and abhorrent to you? It will become strange to your present level of perception, but that changes gradually, as your body does. The energies this new body uses to create life in itself will be different. The requirements of your next step in evolution will cause some changes in the structure of your body, but it will remain a progression of the one you are using now.

However, there is a fear in the mass consciousness of Earth, and most of you share it, that using new energies means you will no longer recognize that form as your own. This is the result of past attempts in Earth's history to use alien structures to move to a new level.

You tend to "get stuck" in your perceptions of what your bodies can do and they can't evolve into the next level. Many times, in the very ancient history of Earth, you have subconsciously invoked a "shock treatment" to help you move your concept of physicality out of its current limitations. Strange beings came to Earth who knew how to use these new energies you wanted to learn to use. They were not aware, at the level of physical consciousness, of the greater purpose they were serving, any more than you were. Their bodies were very different from yours, but they tried to interbreed with you. The results were successful at times, very unfortunate at other times. They sometimes resorted to unique methods to produce successful crossbreeding and births which were very uncomfortable, even very painful to you. But they accomplished their goal. You did begin to use the new energies.

The point is that it was not the experiments in crossbreeding that allowed the integration of the new energies. It was the interaction with these beings who knew how to use them. It was your eventual acceptance of them, at a subconscious level at least, that allowed it. You learned to use the new energies by working and sharing your creativity with those who already knew how to use them. If you could have accepted them as friends in the first place and shared your Earth with them in a way that allowed you to blend your creativity with theirs, you would have saved yourselves a lot of trauma and bad memories.

So now, as beings from other planets, dimensions, universes come to share their use of these new energies which the Earth and you wish to learn to use, you fear that they will try to conquer you and force you to yield to their power and their authority. You fear that they will take away your freedom, your free will. You have learned to fear anyone who is not like yourselves and expect pain and suffering at their hands. Your fear creates painful ways of interacting with different energies — namely aliens who use you for their "experiments." If you have these experiences, you haven't learned to allow your love and acceptance of new things to create the necessary changes within your bodies. Anything that causes your physical form to change has become evil and is feared. This thinking creates the pain and suffering you wish to avoid. Any help that is allowed on higher levels of your consciousness must be done without the cooperation of your physical-level consciousness.

We want to help you understand the new energies from a perspective which will allow you to create the necessary changes in your bodies from the level of thought and feeling. Then they can evolve in a logical, comfortable way. Your fears of what is different block that. We want to help you and the Earth of which you are a part to make those changes from this higher perspective, without the suffering which results from trying to force change from the physical level. We want to help you create a loving, creative interaction with many beings from outside your dimension.

Your soul understands the divine ideal and knows how to make the necessary changes. It can help you integrate the knowledge you need from other races of beings. Let's say your soul is the embodiment of your potential on Earth. It contains the pieces of your fractured knowledge of how to use physical existence. It has integrated them into a useful plan for working at the physical level. It is waiting for you to listen to it and allow it to become part of your physical life. It has access to those parts of your potential that you haven't yet looked at. It understands what your special talents are and how you fit into the Divine Plan.

Many of you are beginning to make a conscious connection with your souls that brings you guidance from it. But you have barely begun to use its understanding, wisdom, and powers of integration. This results partially from the inability of humanity as a whole to connect with Earth as a spiritual being and a source of spiritual power. You have not yet created a conscious interface for connecting your physical consciousness with Earth's creative power as divine love. This means it is not possible to bring the full focus of soul's wisdom and understanding into the physical level. The insights from soul and higher dimensions have an unreality about them that make it difficult to transpose them into information useful at the physical level. Your erroneous thinking patterns do not include soul's. There is no room for input from your soul unless you ask for it and allow it.

This is partly because you try to make everything too difficult. "Act with love," "You are love," or "Be yourself" seem too simple to be useful. When you get a message like that from your higher self, you agree, "That's nice, but how do I do it?" But the inability to make the connection is also a result of the disparity in patterns of thought between soul and Earth. The mass consciousness of Earth is full of negative emotions, fears, and wrong thinking that are not in alignment with the Plan. soul cannot move fully into the physical level until it is cleared of these negative patterns. You must make the realization at the physical level that the ideal pattern is available within every particle of physical existence. You will be moving against the tide of Earth's mass consciousness, but as more and more of you make that realization it becomes part of Earth's thinking patterns. It is easier for others to make the same realization and they, in turn, take you to a higher level of that understanding.

Many of your spiritual teachers have shown you how to do this. As we said before, your Christ took this realization to the highest level yet accomplished on Earth and showed you how. He remains now, at the higher levels of your conscious interaction with the Plan, ready to help you connect to the love that is everywhere around you. When enough of you have been able to do this and maintain that awareness at the physical level, He and many other spiritual teachers will again be a part of physical existence. They will not descend; you will bring the physical level to where they are waiting. There is a certain critical point at which this happens, where enough people on Earth are ready for this realization, and the whole Earth moves forward. It isn't a huge number either, one-tenth of one percent of those in physical existence is all that is required.

Again, it is not the particular physical form you are using that is the divine ideal. The fact that this particular form has allowed you to stretch your use of your full potential to a new level of creativity is what is important. When this form can no longer support growth and you have learned what you need to learn while using it, it is not really the ideal any longer. The form that will allow the new level of expansion becomes the new ideal. The old form becomes a prison which locks you into limitation.

Does this mean you should hate and despise the form you are now using? Certainly not, because it must support you as you make the transition to the next level of creative use of your divine power. The form you now use becomes expanded and transformed, not rejected and cast off. This is the evolved use of your physical body which is, perhaps, the completion of this level of your understanding of yourself as a creator. This form must be loved, supported, and very carefully guided through the transformation. You must learn to accept it as a part of your spiritual self. You must develop very high regard for it because it will allow the expanded spiritual connection into physical existence which you are striving for. The changes it is undergoing will allow you to use your creative power in a new way on Earth.

I told you that we have learned to use unlimited love at the physical level on our planet. This means we have made that realization that allows us to use the divine creative power of our planet as our own. We have built that interface of conscious thought that allows us to see the love of Source flowing through our physical level as well as higher ones. We have learned to use the power of love at the physical level by knowing that it is no less worthy of love, no less divine than any other level. We do not yet have full command of our soul's wisdom and power at the physical level, but we have far more than you do on your Earth. We feel that when we share in your movement toward that perfect alignment with your planet through the Divine Plan, we will take our planet to a new level also.

A clearer understanding of what physical existence really is is needed on your Earth, along with release of the limitations you have placed on your physical selves. I am speaking of the belief that one physical form is more true, more worthy of divine Light than another. This false belief cuts you off from a true realization of what your physical body is and limits your ability to accept the full truth into it, which is necessary to use its full Light potential.

When you accept the sacredness of your physical body, you allow yourself the use of the full creative potential embodied in your cells. You no longer limit your creative potential to what you can achieve from the higher dimensions. Your potential now includes the ability to function in fuller awareness of your divine creative potential while using the physical level. You can understand the Divine Plan in its application and use in physicality. You can invoke and observe the creative process from the physical perspective. You can communicate with others on many levels of awareness, who are working with you within this Plan, while in full consciousness within your physical body. Your physical body becomes as much a participant in the process and contributes to it as much as your mental or spiritual body.

Of course, your emotional body needs to become part of the process also. That awareness is more developed, although also incomplete. As you release the fear of change and new patterns of existence, your emotions take you joyously and enthusiastically along the new paths on which you explore the new level. As you stretch your mind to new levels of understanding, it helps you move your whole being into alignment with the new ideal. As you accept that your soul is indeed as much a part of physical existence as any other level, you have access to its guidance and wisdom. Its spiritual perspective becomes more a part of your thinking, feeling, and acting processes. You have allowed it to bring more of your divine strengths, your special creative abilities, into your life here.

You will have truly expanded into a new use of your creative potential here on Earth. You will have learned to accept Earth as a powerful and unselfish friend who abundantly shares its resources of love and beauty, as it provides a foundation for sharing your resources with all of Earth, all of the beings who derive their physical life from her substance.

This is one step in becoming part of a greater creative group, the one made up of all the cocreator-creators in this universe. This is one step in your return to your true origin, Source. When you can work with this ultimate group, share your creativity and love with it, see that you have played a part in the Divine Plan, you will have achieved your ultimate purpose. We hope that by helping you stretch your ability to interact creatively with Earth now, we will help you move a step closer to that final goal. We aren't here to take you there, just to help you discover your own unique way of getting there. Perhaps our love for you and your Earth can be one of the Lights that guides you to your destination.

11

We have talked a lot about what you need to do to move to the next level of awareness and power. Now I would like to tell you more about what we can do specifically to help you in this. We will also talk about what we are already doing and what we are planning to add to that. It was necessary to establish the correct priorities, because you must, first of all, be willing to work on yourselves. Without that, what we do will not help your understanding and your growth as a creator. We can't do anything for you. We can only help you do it yourself. I cannot repeat that often enough, I think. So many of you are still waiting for someone to come down from the sky and set everything right. We could; and actually that has been tried a number of times by others, but you always rejected the solution because you wanted to do it yourselves.

Many times you have been given a plan to create a situation on Earth that would gather the best of all past experience into an ideal system. But you usually decided to go back yet again into new areas which were not perfected, to learn more. An ideal was reached in ancient Egypt, before recorded history, but it was confined to a very small part of Earth. As it was finished, you tried to extend it beyond that part which could support it. The rest of Earth was not yet developed enough to handle the spiritual energies which it invoked through its connection to the Galactic Center. As you tried to use the flow of Light from there, through your spiritual center in Egypt, Earth seemed to suck out all its power and dissipate the Light that held together that civilization.

The energy structure that supported that system began to be spread out all over the world, taking the balance and central focus with it. The ideal that had been there seemed to deteriorate and dissolve as the knowledge and wisdom, even the Light, seemed to slip away so that no real trace of it was left, only legends and erased memories. That was our job — to erase the memory of what you had done so you would be free to recreate it in a new way.

The spreading out has continued into this millennium. It was not complete until the spark that spread from Egypt to Greece and then to Europe had traveled to the New World in the west and become established there. The decaying relics of Egypt's greatness serve as all that remains of a symbol of what Earth could be. But the symbol lies hidden in them of what you are working toward. They tantalize you with their mysteries and hints of great power and knowledge. They are a link into the Plan which is even now a continuation of what they represent.

But the symbols, the structure, are not the key, not any more. That key is in each of you. As the power of that golden age was distributed around the world, it became a part of all who had had a part in it. The old structure died but left the seeds of its recreation in each of you. These seeds are your desire to create a better world and to be Light yourselves. They are nurtured by your search for knowledge and understanding of that world and yourselves. They are being stimulated into growth now by the Light from the Galactic Center, the Light of the Divine Plan which is the key to the treasure house of knowledge and love in each of you. Everything you knew, all the power you wielded in ancient Egypt, is available to you, waiting to be channeled into the new structure which will create a whole planet that can sustain the inflow of higher energies it uses.

We have been part of your evolution from the beginning. We have helped you work out your purposes on Earth. Our world was complete before yours began so we have no need to focus on ours. We have learned much through working with you, but that is always the way any active existence works. There is always more to learn. By focusing on your world, we have slowed down the "re-run" of our system and tied it to yours in a way that allows us to interact with you. We can comprehend your world, since it is, in a sense, our past. But you cannot, in your physical-plane consciousness, comprehend ours since it is your future which you have not experienced and cannot therefore understand. This causes the communication through the interface between our worlds to be one way up to now.

We can operate consciously in your world without your being aware of us or our world even though they essentially occupy the same space. Our ability to control our world allows us to control yours also. We are not doing that; you are learning to control your own. What we do is the result of your requests from the level of yourselves which can comprehend and communicate with us, that part of yourselves which is aware of the Divine Plan.

There is another type of connection which exists, even at the physical level, and that is the universal energy flow. This universal flow is unlimited so it cannot be restricted to one world or another. Referring back to the symbolism of the hologram, every particle of this universal flow contains something of every other particle within it. We choose to work with this flow as it exists in our system. Since the overall plan for our world is very like yours, even though the time location within it is different, we can focus the structure within the flow and manipulate it mentally. We are working from the highest level of creative knowledge, which you may know as the causal plane. We have studied it, understand it and can consciously manipulate matter from that level. You manipulate matter at that level also, but do not usually do it consciously. You were beginning to understand how to do that in prehistoric Egypt but have forgotten it.

As I said, we erased much of that memory for you. I will tell you how and why. You probably have read or know that when you die, you experience a review of that life. You look at what you accomplished and what you missed. That evaluation becomes a part of the seed atom from which arises your next life — your four bodies and the general outline of experiences you will have. That seed atom then goes to a higher level where it is flooded with the unlimited love and awareness of True self which is the real nurturing of your existence at any level. Sometimes corrections are made here in the pattern of consciousness condensed into that seed atom. As we have a clear focus into the physical level and its needs, as well as the ability to maintain our flow of consciousness into these higher causal levels, we are often asked to make such corrections. Our physical foundation gives the process a continuity of meaning from the causal to the physical level.

Normally, this outside control is not used, but your souls asked for help because, as you tried to use this power, so many times it was in a way that resulted in the destruction of all or most of the life on Earth. Atlantis was only the latest example of that. You recognized that what was needed was clarity of purpose and the ability to work together for a common goal in alignment with the Divine Plan. This clarity can only come when each individual using it is clear of the tendency to give in to negative emotions and selfish purposes. Your Egyptian experience took what was positive in Atlantis and created the ideal on Earth. There was not yet enough of that transforming ability to involve the whole Earth in that "experiment," but you proved that it was possible.

The seed atom is a pattern of Light in which is recorded everything you know. We can go into it and erase specific items, sort of like editing a text on a computer. The pattern that emerges for use in the next life or series of lives bears no trace of the deleted material. If the erasure is carried out properly, the material can be retrieved later, if desired. It is retrieved from your essential Source qualities, your full creative potential. It is possible for you to lose all connection with it so you have to begin again from the beginning to reclaim it, but that is another story of interference from those who are not working within the Plan.

It is extremely difficult to carry out this erasing procedure at all levels, with or without your permission, if you do not consciously allow it. If you doubt your own essential power and free will, if you believe that you can't control your own destiny, you create an opening that allows someone else to come in and create it for you. In other words, you can allow it through ignorance or denial of your free will and Source potential. The opening occurs at whichever level the doubt occurs. Fortunately, you all have higher selves who maintain the knowledge of your true identity for you. There is no doubt there, no openings through which you give away your power to create your own destiny yourself.

Some of you have a few of these openings, or power leaks, at the mental level. There are more at the emotional and physical levels and our purpose is to help you heal them. A life created out of hate, anger, grief, disconnectedness, etc., is full of these openings through which you allow others to control you. We and others have had to step in and provide the control you invited because you were unable to move forward without someone to help you. Like bringing up a child, we have tried to lead you gradually to a maturity which allows you to be responsible for yourselves. Perhaps we have not always been ideal parents, sometimes being too permissive and allowing you to "get into deep trouble," other times being too strict and invoking your rebellion and frustration over not being able to use your own power. But we have always loved you and never lost sight of the creative potential we were nurturing.

But don't get the idea that taking away the memory of your power to control physical matter is in any way punitive. There is a part of yourself which is just as wise and powerful, just as aware of the flow of creation as we are. Your own higher selves are very much our equals in creative power, perhaps greater. In the same way that parents desire their children to be greater than they were, we are supporting your evolution into your full creative potential. Our wisdom is but part of the foundation of yours. Your decision at the higher level to "forget" your knowledge of your power was made to allow yourselves to grow into the ability to use it well.

So you gave up your knowledge of power and literally went back to basics. You spread out all over the Earth, reconnected into the mass consciousness — because Egypt had been placed outside that for the most part — and began to clear it. You took so much of the darkness and negativity of Earth back into yourselves that she was finally plunged into a series of "Dark Ages." There were some bright spots such as the Golden Age of Greek culture and the coming of the Buddha and Jesus Christ, but not until the two world wars were over did you begin to see your way clear of that darkness.

There have been times on Earth, before your recorded history, before even Atlantis or Lemuria, when you used all the power you had. Sometimes you used it well, sometimes not so well. Each era of growth or evolution is succeeded by one that requires you to stretch your concept of your purpose and potential. At the time of Atlantis, there was a stretching beyond what you needed for that time. In a sense you took a greater bite out of your potential use of power than you could chew. If you look at this in the context of a very cosmic view of your development, you were already seeing the needs of the present, very critical period of Earth expansion when you need everything you've got to do the job. But the parts of your potential that you could not integrate into the development of your creativity got you and Earth into a lot of trouble.

At the end of the Egyptian period, you realized that Earth was not ready to receive the knowledge and power you had learned to use. The attempt to continue to use it outside that specialized environment created much frustration and even disaster for you and others. You finally decided, as a group at soul level, to give up that knowledge for a time. However, every experience you have ever had is recorded in your subconscious mind and available to you at the conscious level if you can learn to make the correct associations that will lead you to it.

Many things can be and are buried in your subconscious because you do not wish to deal with them on the conscious level. That does not mean they do not affect your life. Every program you have ever used is running now, perfected or erroneous. When enough of them come together at a common point, a situation symbolic of their common essence manifests in your life. This knowledge and power that you had in Egypt is so closely aligned with your divine purpose and your true identity as a spiritual being that it could not be buried without blocking your spiritual evolution. Erasing your memory of it had to be done in such a way that the ability to use your divine powers remained in undeveloped form along with your innate movement toward developing them. It was something like rewinding a tape to a previous part of the movie and replaying it.

126

Having already developed and used these powers, you have strengthened the means of developing and using them. That remains. So we have the unusual situation of a large group of very creative beings who have learned to tap the source of their unlimited power, but who can no longer remember quite how it was done. Bits and pieces of the knowledge come up, but the whole process never seems to quite come together in a way that can be used for all of Earth.

It is time for you to remember. This is shown by the need for global solutions at a time when there is a rapidly growing source of new energies for creating new solutions. We are here now to help you remember. The solution for the present is different, but the problem must and can be solved with the information and abilities available.

But we have the problem of the confusion of negative thought and emotions still being widely used on Earth. Some of you are becoming quite clear of them and could use your spiritual powers well. Others are far from ready. There is a growing unity in the thoughts and emotions of humanity that is symbolized by the rapid expansion of global communication. You are becoming one, whether you realize it or not. More and more, the thoughts of one group affect the whole Earth very rapidly. If a small group of you begin to use mind power to any significant degree, that will trigger the memory of its use in those who would misuse it and bring about the total conflagration some of you fear. If we bring back the whole pattern of knowledge of the use of your power to any of you, that makes it more available to all.

True, there are a few individuals who can bend spoons and stop watches. But they have not learned to link their minds with others for any significant idealistic purposes. And few have been willing or able to relinquish their will to the Divine Plan. These individuals with special powers serve as reminders of the power that is in each of you. What is needed now is a broad-based clearing of the mass consciousness, so that what you call the "powers of Light" or "Christ Consciousness" are strong enough to outweigh any counter action by those who remain locked in denial of their ability to use unlimited love and their connection to the Divine Plan. Ignorance is waning and the Light of knowledge is growing; you are close to the critical mass needed to direct Light consciously into the Divine Plan. We are bringing back those relinquished memories gradually, hopefully in a way that provides what is needed to progress your spiritual growth as a group involving the whole planet into your next millennium.

So, in addition to gradually helping you to bring back the Light framework for using your power, we are trying to build in some of the connections you need to work together within the Plan. We are helping you to "rewrite your program" for using your power, taking back the memories that had been set aside and adding new openings which allow a clearer connection to the Divine Plan. Is opening to the Plan in this way giving your power to something else? Not really, because this is your plan, remember. You have chosen to share your power within it in order to create your version of what Source intended this creation to be. You have the cooperation of very powerful and experienced cocreator-creators as well as the multitudes of angels and others like yourself. Your power is meant to be shared, given away, if you like, but shared in the way you choose, shared in a way that allows you to grow as creators and evolve the use of your potential.

We create the new pattern of your consciousness in our minds and literally project it directly into yours, visualizing the process by which it becomes part of your conscious thinking. Again, we cannot do it unless you allow us to come in. We can work freely at the levels of higher mind, usually, because your soul is in control there and cooperates with the process. We have had more experience in integrating the spiritual levels into the physical one, so we are serving as teachers of your soul for the procedure. What we do at that level assists your soul in moving this transformation process into the other levels of your mind, the conscious ones. If you have a fairly clear connection with your soul, it can move the new patterns of thinking and feeling down into your conscious mind. If your mind is cluttered with the effects of your erroneous subconscious programming on your daily life, if you are energizing your life with anger, fear, hate, and confusion, there are no openings through which we or your soul can bring the new thought patterns.

That is why meditation is so important now. You need some time to release the noise of your malfunctioning programs and go beyond them to a quiet peaceful place where you can listen for something better. The new patterns require balance and peace to function properly, to allow you to listen for the flow of the Divine Plan so you can find it and flow in harmony with it. That doesn't mean you must meditate so much that you neglect your active life. You need activity on the physical plane, not only to mirror the areas of your programming that need work, but also to practice using the new programs. The ideas you get from your soul, your spiritual teachers and cosmic friends are intended for use in physical existence.

You are learning to listen always to the inner voice while being very active at the physical level. It is not easy, this integration of the spiritual and physical. It requires constant balancing and adjustment in your daily life. What works one day may not work at all in the light of new realizations about self, good or bad. You have to be willing to be constantly aware of what needs to be cleared, reworked, or released within yourself, as well as willing to recognize how to apply new knowledge or enhanced abilities to your life.

We can do more to help you if you are aware of what we are doing at the level of your conscious mind and if you are in agreement with what we are doing. I am trying to show you what we can do, how we do it, and why. We want you to know that we are not trying to manipulate you in any way. We are trying to show you how to resist and reject manipulation by anyone, gods or fellow humans. We want you to realize the full potential of your own godhood, so you become cocreator-creators with the Source, aware of your own power and able to work within the Divine Plan until such a time when you are ready to rest in the knowledge that you have done everything you can to know yourself and your full potential and can then help others learn what you have learned. Or, perhaps, until you become Source yourself.

I said that we occupy the same space you do but in another dimension. We are always close to you. We do not pry into your thoughts, but if you desire some contact or communication with us, we hear you and answer in whatever way seems appropriate. We "filter out" what is inappropriate in the same way we maintain our individual thoughts in our world. If you are willing to allow us to proceed with our part in helping you move to the next level of your self-awareness, you can simply state that to yourself and we will hear you. You will be "answering our call" as you open up your end of the communicative link we are trying to establish into your physical reality, not for physical contact now, but for a conscious awareness of us at the physical level.

You might feel some energy movements around your head or in your auras as we begin to work with your energy structure, if you are sensitive to such things. You might also feel, at times, pressure, heat, tingling, etc., as we begin to work more directly with your cells. If you choose to be very allowing and attentive, the feelings could be very intense, but they will never cause harm or more than temporary discomfort. You can ask for help on special problems if you like, but do not try to direct our energy or force it in any way. Resistance to what we do will cause discomfort or even pain. It is not our intention to cause pain, but if you ask for our contact and energy while you, at the same time, resist it, you create a difficult way of working with us.

We can see quite clearly the new patterns in the Light you wish to align with. We pick out the pattern of the next higher vibrational level in the new energies and mentally visualize it aligning with your cellular structures. You are composed of a multidimensional-dimensional system of crystalline structures which form the pathways for the universal energies that sustain your life and give you your creative vehicle. We can isolate in our mind the patterns that need to be transformed so that you will be able to use a higher vibrational level of that universal flow. We visualize the old pattern in your energy field gradually aligning with the new one and flowing into it. You can do this yourself. Since we have already experienced connecting the visualization with the physical level, we can help you learn to do the same.

Your desire to transform your body into a Light structure that flows in harmony with the divine ideal is the beginning of the process — step one. Step two is to allow yourself to receive the help provided by the Plan that helps you do that. You understand a great deal about your body and how it works. This knowledge, along with your desire to be transformed, becomes the thought energy you put into the process. We intensify the flow and direction of that energy with our visualization. This flow begins to awaken your emotional response. We suggest that you use love in this communicative connection. Send us love as we work with you. It will help you overcome any fears or other negative emotions that may be stimulated by the process.

You have all had experiences where you were apparently helpless as someone did something painful or harmful to your body. These patterns of vulnerability to attack from outside yourself are something we would like to help you release, but you may feel some of the emotions involved in the original experience as it comes up. If you can trust the transformation process and focus as much as possible on the love which motivates it, these positive emotions will replace the negative ones. Don't try to block the pain or fear, anger, hate, etc., just allow it to come up and evaporate as the love washes it out of your energy structure.

We are not working with you at the physical level of your cells only. Each one of your cells, indeed, each of your atoms has a physical, etheric, emotional, mental and spiritual body. These bodies interact and influence each other in the way each uses Light. We will be working on whatever level is necessary to move the transformation process forward. If you need a more secure connection between your spiritual body and the others, we will work on that. If your emotional body is fragmented and weak, we will work to unify and heal it. If your mind has dissociated itself from the rest of the process and thinks it is controlling everything, it will have to be balanced. We will certainly be doing much work on releasing the crystallization of your misperceptions about yourself in your physical cells.

There is a special quality in the Light that is available on Earth now that has a shattering effect. This portion of the Light can be directed into the crystallized patterns in your cells that are inhibiting their alignment with the ideal. That is part of the energy we use to free you of old, outworn energy patterns, rather like a surgeon uses a laser beam. In fact, we recommend that you think of this potentially destructive aspect of Light as one that is preparing the way for the transformed structure. When this powerful element of Light is not constructively utilized, it becomes disruptive to your cells and destroys your body's control systems, the immune system particularly.

You must also be willing, at every level, to release what is no longer needed. If one part of you is hanging on to what another part is trying to release, the subconscious sees the process as destructive and creates injury or illness. If you keep releasing what is not needed, you will eventually get to the root of the misperception or fractionating. In the past, the process might have taken many lifetimes. Now, the energies are moving so fast, you may have to look very quickly to even see what it was. But, you will be able to clear out even the deepest issues in yourself if you persist, trust the process and use love to connect with yourself and those who are willing and ready to help you.

We have not been looking for interaction with you in order to impose any "cosmic sanctions" or will upon you. We are all part of the same Plan. We agreed at its inception to work together, each in our own way, to evolve the potential of the whole. Since each of us contains the whole within us, we all grow together. Sharing in the spirit of unlimited love never creates loss of any kind. On the contrary, once you have passed over the difficulty of letting go, you will find you have lost nothing and gained much. There is no way to know this until you experience it. Life is an opportunity to constantly let go of yourselves at every level and allow the accomplishments from there evolve into the opportunities of the new one. As you move from one level to the next, you will find new ways to use your well-earned knowledge and new ways to expand it.

There is nothing we desire more than that you should exceed us in the development of your power and love. We want your world to be better than ours, more diverse, more expansive in its use of love. The potential is there, in your hearts, bursting forth as Light. Your Earth is the ideal garden in which to grow many new ways of creating with love. Perhaps, one day, ours will become united with yours in one expanded dimension where love is indeed unlimited.

12

Ranoash Answers Questions

In the first chapter you seemed to come from a view point of being very physical and not so highly developed, having many of the same problems we have. In the later chapters you seemed to be coming from a much more highly evolved point where the fighting and dissension and misunderstandings of self no longer existed. Can you explain that?

Yes. I would be happy to. We are multidimensional beings. As I told you, we remained in our physical flow. We retained the physical existence that we had created, while at the same time we also existed at higher levels. We are multidimensional beings just as you are. The difference is that we can see those dimensions within ourselves all at once. We have integrated what we were with what we are now and what we are as a whole. We have gone past the integration of ourselves, our personal evolution and our personal involvement with development into sharing with the group. We share our experiences with the group as a whole, so that it is as if the whole experiences everything that each individual experiences and has the benefit of that experience. We have all learned, then, from what the others have done.

At the time we were experiencing it at the most physical and most limited levels we did not understand this and we suffered a great deal, just as you are. Now that we have evolved to the point where we can go beyond ourselves to find the unity of ourselves with the whole, we no longer feel that separation but we still have the knowledge that we gained in that state. This is partly what we want to share with you: the ability to stretch yourselves through the limitations of physicality and individuality to being able to share your learning with the whole and being able to learn from what the whole has experienced both as individuals and as a whole. So we can bring many perspectives, many dimensional viewpoints, to bear on your problems. We can use our experience from any level of perception to aid you in understanding yours.

In the past you haven't been able to understand anything beyond your own personal viewpoint, beyond your third-dimensional perceptions. But now as you are expanding your minds and as you begin to see something beyond yourselves, then the opportunity for us to aid you in bringing what appears to be beyond yourself into yourself as a part of your own expansion is available to us.

In the past, every bit of help we gave you had to come as if from outside. And since you have been and still are to some extent very tightly locked into your own individuality, your own flow, and trying to control your own destiny from a personal viewpoint, it has been very difficult. It has been very difficult to bring anything from the outside to you, for you to open to any of help we can give, because you see that as interference.

It has been said by many, and there is some truth to this viewpoint, that the Earth has been closed because of the amount of discord and even evil that has been here. From a somewhat different perspective you could say that it was the focusing on solving those problems, on resolving darkness into Light, on transforming that darkness, that caused you to set limits around yourselves through which no one could come. In other words, you have set the boundaries, you have chosen the focus on negativity and you have chosen to do it by yourselves, not because you did not wish help but because your focus limited your reality to the point where you could no longer touch the help that was there for you. As you focused in more and more on the problems and the difficulties, the lines of love from your hearts were directed more and more intensely into negativity so they were not available to provide the receptive flow you needed to bring in the Light that would solve the problems, the Light that would provide the flow that would move the darkness, move the stuckness, move the negativity, and transform it into Light.

You can look at this as an era from your viewpoint but it has served the purpose of allowing you to focus very clearly on exactly what the problem is. Now that you have finally decided to release the problem and begin to resolve it, the flow is beginning to come back, and it will help you to transform that darkness into Light, to solve the problem of evil on the Earth and to bring in the love necessary to solve the problems that are there. It took a great deal of will and force to grapple with this negativity, this evil. You had to reach out, forcibly grasp it and take it into yourself because since you, yourself, were being Light you really did not want to flow into what was darkness, what had not been accepted as Light. But your will drove you on, deeper and deeper into the darkness so that you could take it into yourself and solve the problems of how to use it as Light. You have to decide, each one of you by yourself, how to transform the darkness in you into Light, into love and into creative flow.

Sometimes it takes a war or a blood bath to transcend the idea of releasing negativity, releasing evil. The period of war that has spread throughout this century has been a bleeding that has released the forces of evil and has begun to move the stuckness and negativity that pervaded the Earth for so long, thus allowing it to begin to move. The movement itself then begins to pull Light in and begins to allow the flow of love which brings the solutions, which brings the Light that allows you to see that the problems are solvable. The Light shows you there is a creative potential here, there is love you can use to recreate the Earth in a peaceful and more beautiful, more productive image.

Well, we have integrated all of that and have solved all of the problems to our satisfaction. We have taken it all to another level, into a wholeness, yet we have retained the specifics within ourselves. This is not the way evolution normally proceeds but, as I said earlier, we have chosen to spin the whole history of our evolution out, and we maintain it now as a guide or as an example of how your evolution can develop. It is a sort of stairway that is all laid out for you. That doesn't mean that we can climb the stairs for you. It simply means that it is there as a guide and that we can advise you on certain aspects of your own evolutionary process.

At the same time you are doing your own thing, you are going into things much more deeply than we did. Therefore, you have come up against problems that we did not experience or did not experience as deeply. But we have been able to maintain the vision of the goal and to hold the purpose strongly in mind so that when you lose the purpose, our holding it will move you back into it, even though you have forgotten where you are going.

We are not saying that without us you would not be able proceed or that you have any need whatsoever of what we are doing for you. But we are saying that we are here if you need us, and in the wholeness of consciousness it is not possible to separate yourself from the whole of reality. Every part of the whole is influenced by every other part, and the more your awareness expands into the new dimensions, the more you will begin to see how much you support those who are having difficulty and how much those who are smoothly moving toward the goal of integrating all into a focus of love are able to, in a sense, pull you into their flow.

There is nothing wrong with allowing someone to help you. On Earth you have a sort of compulsion to do things yourself because you have the idea that is the way to learn, and that is true. But in another way of thinking, you don't do anything by yourself. Everything that you accomplish is done as part of the whole and it is impossible to separate yourself from it. You cannot separate the fruits of your goals from others' and you cannot separate the loss of or separation from your goals from their effect on the whole. When we work with you and when we consciously send energy into your experiential flow we use whatever part of our own experience relates most closely to what you are doing because then the frequencies of that experience will blend more harmoniously and more powerfully with yours. The frequencies must be similar in order for our frequency, our flow, to pull you into the flow of movement toward the goal of the universe or into the ideal flow of the Creator's Plan. So when I speak of times or levels of experiencing in which we sound like we were in as much trouble as you are, we are using the vibration of that experience to show you the way out of yours, to show you the resolution we have discovered, to show you the movement toward the vibration of love that carried us to a greater understanding of how to use our energies effectively for the purposes of the Divine Plan rather than for the purposes of negativity, selfishness and separation. Even while we remembered and focused on the other level of experiencing that was less than perfect, we maintained at the same time the accomplishment, the resolution of that experience. We maintained the consciousness of wholeness that we had reached, and we maintained the awareness of reaching that goal and resolving all difficulties.

Is this a backward step for us and does it take us out of the perfect consciousness that we have achieved? No, not really, because we realize that all parts of ourselves are divine, that the experiencing and searching are part of the goal, a necessary part of the goal, and that the goal does not exist in a fully developed sense unless we have explored all the parameters we could create within us. The more of these we explore and resolve, the more we know about the wholeness once we have reached it. So we learn from what you do and although your experience has perhaps gone deeper into confusion, separation and negativity than ours did, it is not so much different. We still understand it and our ability to maintain the concept and the awareness of perfection and wholeness can serve as a guide. It has served as a guide for your Earth.

What is your relationship to us?

We are your older brothers; we are your fathers and mothers; we are your guides. In a sense, we are your conscience. We are also very much a part of yourselves that you have not yet integrated. Now does this mean that we are an aspect of your higher self? In some cases, yes. In some cases your higher self, your God-self, is existing as one of us in our dimension and as one of you in your Earth dimension. In other cases we simply serve as an example, a very close relative, a loving uncle or aunt, perhaps, who understands you very well, has watched you grow and wishes to support and help you, one who has the wisdom of age and experience that would be useful to you in your place within the evolutionary flow right now.

We want you to learn very clearly the importance of your physical existence and your physical body. It took eons to develop your physical body to the perfection you have available right now, a body that can feel and experience and flow at the physical level and yet is reaching to connect into the highest levels of consciousness while remaining aware at the physical level. Your bodies are what give your soul, your highest God-self, your Monad, the ability to experience physicality and to learn from it. But until you learn to make the inner connections with your highest self, it does not gain the advantage of your experience. So all of the thousands and millions of years during which life has been evolving on Earth are only now reaching a climax as you learn to recognize within your-selves the divine spark that began the movement toward conscious-ness and mastery of physicality and that has allowed the growth of the mechanism that is your physical body.

Life did not arise on Earth spontaneously, as your scientists would like to think; at the same time, you were not dumped there by some alien agency, as others of you might like to think. There was a gradual development in which your consciousness, your higher self and the creative aspects of yourself (which were involved in developing the physical body) took part. As a group, you took part in the formation of life. You took part in the gathering of life force into small particles. You took part in the stimulation of those smallest life forms and watched them and cared for them and stimulated their development. As life gradually became more and more complex, help came from outside Earth in the sense that it came from outside the physical level of existence, even though at the same time the potential for life was always present within the Earth, just as your potential for life was always present within you.

The key to your evolution at the physical level is your DNA. In your DNA molecules are recorded the whole history of the evolution of life on Earth as well as the potential of the physical on Earth. At specific stages in Earth's development there is an expansion within the physical form that brings into play more of the potential in the DNA and begins to use it to expand the ability of the physical form first to experience the physical existence and then to begin to alter it, control it and, finally, to master it. The stimulus for this comes from within the Earth, from the potential that was placed within Earth at the time of its creative inception. It is defined by the purpose outlined by the Creator and by you as the Creator. At specific times the need to expand brings in great rushes of energy; increases of Light are available and this Light contains the key which, in a sense, turns on the next level of use of your DNA. The key is not physical. It is given at higher levels of consciousness, at the mental level which then creates the key at the emotional level; the emotional level creates the key that activates the change at the physical level.

The emotional level is the level of astral consciousness where form and Light take shape for you. It's sometimes a shadowy level of consciousness where dreaming and imagination occur. But if enough of you concentrate on and focus on the same reality, then it begins to become real for you at a physical level. This physical reality then takes whatever shape makes the most sense to your mind at the time. At the present level of your technological, mental way of thinking, a spaceship that beams from another planet seems to fit well into the flow of what your subconscious mind can accept and use. So in a sense, you, at the physical level, shape the key that is activating the next level of your enlightenment, your growth and expansion toward enlightenment. What I am saying is that if something else made more sense to you than your present visions and knowledge of what you call UFOs, your key would be something entirely different.

So you invoke the key that unlocks the potential and begins to move you forward. Your invocation brings in the Light in whatever form makes sense to you and that becomes real for you at the physical level as you accept the reality of this change into your physical bodies.

At the same time, the tendency of physical matter when left without life, without the guidance of the spiritual connection, is simply to deteriorate and die, go back into a less complicated state, break down into the simplest elements available. It's consciousness and the will to create that hold your body in complex biochemical form, and it is your will to evolve that allows these biochemical and biological systems to become more and more complex. So the increase of Light becomes the connection that allows your bodies to grow and evolve.

At the same time, the physical elements of which your bodies are composed have a will of their own. They haven't been enlightened to the extent they realize they are a part of this grand organization, this grand plan, and they have a resistance to becoming separate from their individual identities. They cling to them and it is your job as a master of your physical body to help the physical matter within your body to release that tendency to want to remain in the simplest state and to help it connect with the complexity of the Divine Plan which allows you to mature and develop as spiritual beings. You have mastered the Light within to the point where you can maintain your physical bodies for a certain amount of time. But to the extent that you allow your energy to be fractured into the negative expression of experiences, then you do not bring into your body the full flow of Light that would allow it to maintain itself past a specific length of lifetime. Your inability to maintain a completely integrated under-standing of your wholeness allows separation into specific areas of stuckness or negative emotions which create a dissonance, prevent-ing the self from vibrating in unity. When it does not vibrate in unity, it does not have access to the flow of the creative Light that is trying to organize it into the perfected being that you can and will eventually become.

Now each one of you has help from what you call outside of yourself that will help you recognize and clear out or integrate these separated parts of yourself that are causing you to experience pain and aging and that tear apart your physical body instead of healing it and moving it to the next level of frequency of Light. When you do allow integration within yourself, when you do release the negative emotions that keep parts of your creative flow stuck in specific areas where they cannot support your alignment with the ideal, then you begin to align more with the flow of the ideal. You begin to bring more of your creative force into creating the ideal and you are able to vibrate to frequency greater than the frequency radiation of your own DNA. We and those who work with us do whatever we can to help you to make the alignment with your own DNA life codes and to release whatever is within yourself that resists that alignment.

This is involves some interaction with what you consider to be beings who operate outside of your own reality because your reality does not yet include expansion to the next levels. There is not a system of social structure, political structure, educational structure and so forth that does support such expansion. It is all designed to maintain the status quo, to keep you at the level where you are. This is beneficial to some extent but, of course, it has disadvantages. So the enlightened part of yourself, your soul and your higher self, which you are trying to become more involved with in your life, are antagonistic to the other part of yourself that is clinging to the status quo, the present level of achievement, as the only way to maintain your existence.

We come in harmony, in alignment with the will of your higher self. We come as aspects of Light that are trying to become a part of your physical existence. Your physical body sees that as an intrusion and as a violation of your right to maintain the level of existence that you have chosen at the physical level. The more you choose alignment with the will of higher self, the more you invoke this help which seems to be outside yourself. Eventually there is a point when you realize that what seems to be outside yourself is really in harmony with your will. It really is an aspect of your divine will and is serving to bring you closer to the perfection that your soul requires to exist at the physical level. Those of you who have experienced great psychological and emotional trauma because of remembered experiences with UFOs and abductions are those who are clinging most desperately to the physical body as it exists right now. When you can transcend the idea that the physical body is what defines you and transcend it within every cell of your being — so that every cell recognizes that it is part of a flow toward the unity and perfection of the single ideal or purpose — then your body will begin to adjust to the changes that are taking place. It will be able to release more rapidly and easily the stuckness and negativity that is within you. You will be able to use the energy for positive purposes rather than negative ones. Then the transformation process becomes not one of being used by abductors but one of cooperating fully with the growth and use of soul energy within your body and the transformation of yourself into a being with expanded consciousness who can use the higher frequencies of Light which the Earth is calling for to bring about its own evolution in consciousness.

It is not a simple thing to integrate greater and greater quantities of Light into your physical life. The physical body resists it. It has to learn how to use it. It has to learn how to direct it. It has to learn how to move it in a balanced way to all parts of your body and all levels of your awareness, understanding and consciousness. It has to learn to balance the flow in many different ways through the mental, physical and emotional levels, as well as the spiritual, and it has to balance it. It was never intended that you should isolate yourselves within your physical consciousness but that you would have available to you all the help you needed to guide you through your journey into the darkness of the Earth's creative potential and back out into a greater awareness of your own creative abilities.

Remember that we are not here to tell you how to do it or to force you to do anything our way. We are here simply to support you in doing what you have already decided at a higher level to do, to help you to achieve your own plans, your own purposes. They are not so different from ours, although you do not always understand them at the physical level. Our purpose now is to help you come to terms with those parts of yourselves that want to move forward very rapidly and want to bring great quantities of Light into the Earth. We want to help you to create the bodies that will allow you to do that. We want to help you to master your physical bodies and to tame the beast that rages within you and cries for freedom and independence. We do not wish to take freedom and independence away from you, but in order to achieve what you wish, you must give up your freedom and independence and align with the flow of the ideal that is there for you. In that way you will gain freedom and independence to a degree that you had never imagined. You will gain through your surrender the ability to create yourself and your Earth in new and better ways, according to a higher ideal.

Do you control us in anyway?

Well, let's look at it this way. When you have a child too young to understand how to control his or her own life, if you love that child then you set the controls and limits that allow him to grow into responsibility for determining his own life. It would be unconscionable for a parent to simply turn away from the child because it did not know how to control itself to fit into the format of the society it is living in. It's the parents' responsibility to teach the child how to fit into the structure and how to live in a way that supports itself as well as the structure that keeps the system organized.

The difference between this example and your life on Earth is that is that you have determined from a higher level what the structure will be and exactly what you want to learn in your lifetime. We simply are responsible for maintaining the structure that allows you to accomplish the goals you have already chosen. When you leave that higher level where you determine your goals and go to the physical level, you often lose the memory of the goal and the best way to achieve it. So we define the limits of your life and the way you use them at the physical level in order to help you accomplish your goals and make the progress you are looking for in each lifetime.

Now you have to understand that every experience you have on Earth is carried in some way in your cellular memory. It is encoded into the DNA at many levels in the way your body functions and reproduces itself. The specific parts of the body then manifest according to their functions in supporting life. At the normal rate of evolution the forms you encode into your DNA, which determine certain ways of responding to life, serve you well and maintain a consistent flow in the learning process. They hold you to your task and keep you focused on the lessons you need to learn. As you slowly resolve all the problems and as you slowly release the need for the misprogramming, the DNA is restructured at the end of every lifetime. But on Earth, for the past five thousand years particularly, you have chosen to accelerate the normal flow of evolution so that the restructuring at the end of every lifetime is often not enough to allow you to make the progress you are looking for; so restructuring is required during the life. All the time you are not awake at the physical level is needed to heal and restructure a new program in your DNA to account for the learning process that is occurring every day of your life. When you have the ideal connection of all parts of yourself into the highest levels of consciousness or into the ideal plan, then the reprogramming takes place automatically, without any help from the outside, so everything works as it should. There is a flow of releasing and restructuring. But when specific parts of yourself become cut off from the ideal and from the governing control of your higher self then these parts of yourself are not able to heal themselves. They require intervention at the physical level because the flow of information or healing or reprogramming is cut off.

There are many groups that work with Earth; this is because at certain points, Earth became so cut off and locked within this physical perspective that it was in imminent danger of dying and becoming disconnected from the whole flow of the rest of the cosmos. It was releasing itself from the flow of the Divine Plan. Various groups began to work on solutions to this problem and began to work with Earth and humanity to reconnect and correct the misprogramming that did not allow the ideal to be a part of the flow at all levels. These beings had their own purposes and they also shared certain problems with the Earth. Their perspective allowed them a somewhat clearer vision of how to solve the problems which they shared, and therefore they were allowed to interact with humanity so they could begin working together to correct the problems that existed on Earth. Not all of the beings maintained an absolutely clear connection into the ideal but most were somewhat more aware of the common universal goals than was Earth itself at the physical level. Some of these beings, through their interaction with physical existence, became almost as disconnected from the higher levels as Earth itself. And yet the flow of experience tied you all together and you continued to work on the problems.

In some cases this required interaction from still other beings who came to help both groups, once they had become involved in the misuse of the cosmic ideal. These other groups had, for the most part, solved their own problems and were simply tying up the last threads of their experience of the physical level by helping Earth to reconnect with its original purpose.

Now we will say again that the ideal for the physical body is for the highest levels of consciousness to interact with physical level. The nature of physical existence was that it tended to cut off the flow of this information. It was not intended that your body should reject higher energies or be damaged by them, but the misprogramming and the misinterpretation by faulty DNA do not allow you to use the higher energies that bring information from the highest levels of consciousness, and this is where the restructuring and the repair are taking place now. If you are able to maintain that soul connection with every aspect of yourself then you do not need help from the outside. The connection flows and reprogramming occurs as misperceptions are released. But for most of you on Earth a release or an understanding on the mental level does not guarantee the release of that information at the physical level because there is a cutoff; you do not see the physical level as part of the higher levels of consciousness or of the higher level of yourself. So intervention is needed in the form of technology that can transform the higher levels of information or consciousness into energy codes that can be utilized by the physical level. Some of this can be done through the mental or even the emotional levels but work done on the etheric level requires a physical contact.

Most of the help you get with your body from those outside yourself is done at the etheric level and therefore it does not require full consciousness at the physical level. It can occur during the day when your mind is occupied by concerns of your third-dimensional existence. But at night when you release your third-dimensional consciousness and relax your mind so that other levels of awareness are there for you, then you begin to be aware of what's going on on the etheric level and you become aware of something other than what you know to be yourself that is intervening in the function of your physical body. When you are locked into the fear that the physical is the most important part of yourself then this becomes an intrusion and an experience to be feared and rejected. Yet your higher self is saying that this is what is needed, that it's part of the flow of purpose for this physical existence to try to release the old pattern of isolation on this physical level and reconnect all parts of self into one continuous flow of awareness. So the intervention that seems to come from outside comes as a request from your own higher self which you do not necessarily have knowledge of at the physical level. It is unfortunate that there is no way to make this conversion into higher energy an easy one for you, but the conflict really comes from within yourself. The disconnected parts of yourself are battling against the connection that will enable you to make the changes that will allow you make the transformation process an easy one.

The parts of yourself that are aware and connected with your higher purpose are bringing every bit of will and energy to bear on bringing you into alignment with the ideal. This causes great conflict within itself which is reflected as conflict with what appears to be coming from outside yourself. I wish there were some way I could make this more real for you at the physical level; but until you can accept that you are totally in control of your environment, that you totally create your reality, there is no way I can help you to accept this intervention and this help which are very necessary now, even for your survival. Earth has become so cut off that since life cannot exist if it doesn't receive the nourishment of the flow of the Creator's love that supports all life and all existence, you cannot exist without help from the outside. You have cut yourself off from that flow and therefore are strangling life within you when you do not see that the physical body is a continuous flow of energy with the highest levels of

Source and the purest love that are present in the universe.

Are your physical lives being controlled by something outside yourself? Yes. Is that something outside of yourself separate from you? No. It is a result of your own higher consciousness seeking to make a reconnection with the totality of what you are. It is an attempt by all levels of self that are connected in any way with the ideal to bring the whole of your being into the flow of that ideal. When you can learn to look at your physical self and your physical flow of experiencing and even of thinking and feeling from the perspective of the ideal then you will be able to give that part of yourself the love and care it needs to come back into the wholeness of your being. Then you will be able to be your own teacher, your own healer, and outside intervention will not be necessary because you will have realized that what is seeking to interact is your own higher purpose. It is the result of your own higher purpose.

How are you related to the abduction phenomenon?

We are the overseers of the guides; you might say we are the higher authority on intervention from other levels of existence or from Earth itself, outside the three-dimensional frame of experience (everything related to your three-dimensional domain of understanding, as you see it.) Due to your focus into physical existence and the necessity for limiting your understanding in order to accomplish specific goals and specific levels, you are not able to see what goes on outside that focus, beyond your third-dimensional approach. Now that the dimensions are thinning and you are becoming aware of what is going on, it appears that there is interference coming from outside your frame of reference because you are not accustomed to dealing with this. As you begin to integrate more parts of yourself and as you begin to flow more easily with the unifying aspects of your soul energy, then you will begin to understand more that what appears to be outside interference is really a broader understanding of what you are, and it is really a bringing together of aspects of your own consciousness.

It is our job to see that this proceeds in a somewhat organized way and in a way that is acceptable to you. Things must not occur so fast that you are overwhelmed by more than you can integrate at one time. At the same time, the resistance to flow that is part of the physical level has required a certain prodding or encouragement from outside in order to get moving things that had just about come to a complete stand still. So we have been orchestrating, you might say, the change that is occurring on Earth. We are orchestrating the amount of energy that you integrate from outside aspects of yourself in your attempt to reach some sort of wholeness. As the energies approaching Earth now are accelerating so rapidly, your physical selves need encouragement to continue increasing your alignment with them. So in that sense we are prodding you into higher consciousness. We do not do all the work ourselves. But in cases where there is much what you call karma to be worked out with beings from other extraterrestrial groups or other-dimensional beings and at the same time a great flowing alignment within self, there must be a very careful balancing and monitoring of the interactions between you so that you are allowed to solve your problems and at the same time make the necessary adjustments within your DNA and your alignment with the Light. Without careful monitoring it is quite possible for the rapid resolution of the karma to overwhelm you or, let's say, for the rapid reappearance of your karma and the necessity to immerse yourself in it and solve it now, finally, to overwhelm you and plunge you back into darkness. That extremely cut-off state causes you to lose all the gain that you have made in your alignment with the ideal and the realignment of your DNA.

If you want more. . .
we offer the following!

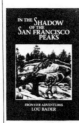
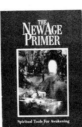

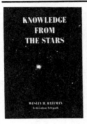

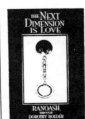

BOOK MARKET

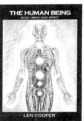

TO ORDER SEE FORM AT BOTTOM OF PRECEDING PAGE.

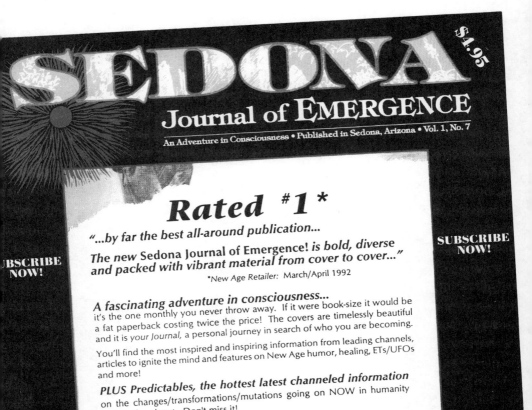